PE

Vanessa

Wensley Clarkson has been a writer and investigative journalist all his working life. He is the author of more than thirty non-fiction true crime books and two novels, which have been published in eighteen countries across the world and sold more than one million copies. He has also written for ITV's *The Bill* as well as directed, written and produced a TV documentary on the British criminal mastermind Kenneth Noye. His latest original movie screenplay, *The Last Word*, is scheduled to go into production in the spring of 2010. He has homes in London and Granada, Spain.

Vanessa

A Portrait of Evil

WENSLEY CLARKSON

PENGUIN BOOKS

PENGUIN BOOKS

Published by the Penguin Group
Penguin Books Ltd, 80 Strand, London WC2R ORL, England
Penguin Group (USA) Inc., 375 Hudson Street, New York, New York 10014, USA
Penguin Group (Canada), 90 Eglinton Avenue East, Suite 700, Toronto, Ontario, Canada M4P 2Y3
(a division of Pearson Penguin Canada Inc.)
Penguin Ireland, 25 St Stephen's Green, Dublin 2, Ireland (a division of Penguin Books Ltd)
Penguin Group (Australia), 250 Camberwell Road, Camberwell, Victoria 3124, Australia
(a division of Pearson Australia Group Pty Ltd)
Penguin Books India Pvt Ltd, 11 Community Centre, Panchsheel Park, New Delhi – 110 017, India
Penguin Group (NZ), 67 Apollo Drive, Rosedale, North Shore 0632, New Zealand
(a division of Pearson New Zealand Ltd)
Penguin Books (South Africa) (Pty) Ltd, 24 Sturdee Avenue, Rosebank,
Johannesburg 2196, South Africa

Penguin Books Ltd, Registered Offices: 80 Strand, London WC2R ORL, England

www.penguin.com

First published 2010
2

Set in 12.5/14.75 pt Garamond MT
Typeset by Ellipsis Books Limited, Glasgow
Printed in Great Britain by Clays Ltd, St Ives plc

ISBN: 978-0-141-04912-0

www.greenpenguin.co.uk

'Those of us that are privileged by the birth of children know that they are the greatest treasure, almost a gift beyond price. Hard-working parents put great effort into their nurture. Part of that is to entrust them and put this treasure into the hands of others. The breach of that trust by this person in such a position of responsibility to me is almost unimaginable. The parents of those abused must be so fundamentally shaken at this unspeakable wickedness.'

Bishop of Plymouth, the Right Reverend John Ford

Contents

Author's Note

Highlighting Vanessa George's difficult childhood in this book in no way excuses her heinous crimes. Trying to blame her past for the present is an obvious route to take but that is definitely not my intention. Vanessa George has no defence for the crimes she committed, but it is important to explain how she came to be in such an appalling 'place' so that perhaps other similar catastrophes might be avoided in the future. So when you read this account of Vanessa George's life and crimes remember this is not an excuse for who she is. It is who she is.

To avoid confusion – apart from during descriptions of her childhood and when she is referred to directly by acquaintances – I have called Vanessa George either 'Vanessa' or later, after her marriage, for the most part simply 'George'. The way her name has been used in no way reflects any sympathy for her crimes. Instead, it is a realistic way to avoid confusion in this book.

Quotations from written material appear, with few exceptions, without the editorial '(sic)'. When it seems that a word was inadvertently missing, it has been added for the sake of clarity. Mistakes in punctuation, grammar and spelling have been corrected in certain instances, but in others it was felt that retaining an error helped convey the flavour of a document and the style of the person being quoted. Some names of sources have been changed or omitted because many of those linked to Vanessa George greatly fear her retribution. Many scenes have been constructed through available documents and allegations provided to this author. A lot of the people I spoke to during this investigation agreed to talk because they felt that breaking the silence surrounding the issue of such a difficult subject might one day help the innocent victims and better protect our children in the future.

Wensley Clarkson, January 2010

Illustrations

Vanessa as a young girl. (INS News Agency Ltd)

Vanessa's parents, Sylvia and Roger. (Barry Medway)

An advertisement for the band with which Sylvia, Vanessa's mother, sang. (Barry Medway)

The house in Crozier Road, Plymouth, where Vanessa and her mother moved shortly after her parents split up. (Wensley Clarkson)

The obituary which carried news of Vanessa's mother's death. (Barry Medway)

Snapshots of Vanessa with her family at Christmas. (Barry Medway)

Andrew George with his daughters, Pearl and Grace. (INS News Agency Ltd)

Just days after Vanessa's arrest, Andrew emerges from his Plymouth home a broken man after an alleged suicide attempt. (SWNS)

The house of horrors from which Vanessa sent thousands of explicit emails, photographs and texts to paedophile Colin Blanchard. (Wensley Clarkson)

The social-networking site Facebook offered Vanessa an exciting and harmless escape from her work, but also introduced her to Allen and Blanchard. (SWNS)

To her friends, Vanessa appeared to be a bubbly, fun-loving woman with a heart of gold. (SWNS)

Shamed. Vanessa attempts to shield her face as she arrives at court in a police van after her arrest. (PA Photos)

Outside the court, public outrage and disgust bordered on violence, as furious parents and members of the community gathered to catch a glimpse of Vanessa. (PA Photos)

Meanwhile, the media was in a state of frenzy. (Getty Images)

Vanessa George, Angela Allen and Colin Blanchard: three faces of despicable evil. (SWNS)

Every effort has been made to trace copyright holders. The publishers will be glad to rectify in future editions any errors or omissions brought to their attention.

Prologue

Interview room, Charles Cross Police Station, Plymouth, Devon, Tuesday, 9 June 2009, 1.44 a.m.

An overweight woman in her late thirties/early forties sits at a wooden table opposite two police detectives. Her heavy, jowly facial features show little emotion as she answers questions in an almost matter-of-fact fashion, as if she is discussing something perfectly normal.

POLICE: Can you introduce yourself.

VG: I'm Vanessa George.

POLICE: Do you want to have a solicitor present?

VG: No, I'm all right, thank you.

POLICE: You remember when we first came [to your home] . . . You said 'I know what it's about, I don't want my husband to know' and then we cautioned you . . .

VG: Mmm.

POLICE: And I said 'I believe that you've sent images' and you said, 'no, just photos of children', 'you know I'm going to have to arrest you' and you said, 'I got suckered in big time, is it Colin Blanchard?', and I said 'who is Colin Blanchard?', 'it doesn't matter' you said. You were then arrested on suspicion of making and distributing images, indecent images of children.

VG: Mmm.

POLICE: And you were also arrested on suspicion of sexual assault by penetration.

VG: Yeah.

POLICE: To which you said 'it wasn't penetration'. You said 'there's nothing in my house, my phone is in my pocket, I've been suckered in big time'.

And then your husband came down and you said to him 'basically I got befriended by a bloke, who said I want you in my life and I took photos of children for him, I'm sorry'.

At half past midnight you said 'I knew this would happen, I can't believe what I've done' . . . and then you gave me your Samsung mobile phone which we have here, and you said to me 'they don't know anything about it' – referring to your family.

VG: Right.

POLICE: You said 'I'll give you my other mobile' . . .

VG: Wasn't.

POLICE: You said, 'I'm disgusted with myself, I can't believe what I've done, I love children'.

VG: I love working with children.

POLICE: 'I love working with children'. You then told me it was a pay-as-you-go phone – you called it your fun phone.

VG: Mmm.

POLICE: Also while we were there, you said you had several email accounts . . .

VG: Yes.

POLICE: I think probably the easiest thing now is for you just to tell us what's happened from the start.

VG: I was on Facebook about, well about five, six months ago and I went on the thing called 'Are You Interested?' And, um, you just click on people and like have a flirt and chat and things like that and there was one I like clicked and I thought nice looking you know and whatever and we just started, I can't even remember, you know he was like 'Hi, how are you, did you have a nice day, blah blah blah' and we started talking on there. Then we added each other as friends and then, he just said 'oh have you got an MSN account?' and I don't think I did at the time, like I must have had one but not. So I just set up one and said 'oh there it is' and we just used to talk on there. Um, and he just said things like 'what's your fantasies?' and things like that and of course you sort of like make up bits and things and like he said he was abused when he was little and I said 'oh that's awful' and he goes 'no, it was really nice'. So I thought 'oh, I got a kinky one here', so I'll play along with it.

POLICE: Mmm.

VG: And I just like played along and like, you know, like typing in things like that and I don't even know how it got to the point of where I think he laughed and, you know, when they say 'oh I want you in my life', um, 'I've told my mum about you' and things like that and I don't know, cos

I never really asked him like, what 'have you got money' or nothing cos I wasn't, you know, it was just a bit of attention to be quite honest and I don't even know how it got onto it, but he sort of said, I said to him like, 'I work in the nursery' and things like that and it was just, he sort of said if you, you know, 'if you take some pictures' or something like that and I've gone 'yeah all right then', and I said 'well what would you do for me if I done that for you?', like joking . . .

POLICE: Yeah.

VG: . . . and I said 'you'll have to put a ring on my finger to make me do things like that' and it was like 'Mmm' . . . So then I did and then of course the more photos you take the more you get back, you know, in interest.

POLICE: Sort of feeding him type.

VG: Yeah, but it was attention back.

POLICE: When you say take photographs, what do you mean?

VG: Taking photos of children.

POLICE: In what way?

VG: Oh, their parts.

POLICE: Do you want to tell me what, if you can think of the first photograph you took.

VG: Most probably just a little girl.

POLICE: Can you remember who it was?

4

VG: No, I can't.

POLICE: Where was this?

VG: In the nursery in the toilets . . . Take them in for nappy changing . . . And then I'd do it then.

POLICE: I can see you are upset.

VG: I'm fuming with myself really, I am because it's like the epitome isn't it, it's like absolutely disgusting and I knew, you know, you just think it's wrong, but . . .

POLICE: You're being very brave this evening, OK and thank you.

VG: Mmm.

POLICE: So how many pictures do you think you've taken?

VG: Most probably lots.

POLICE: How many's lots?

VG: I wouldn't honestly say but it was . . .

POLICE: Hundred, two hundred?

VG: I don't know, it wasn't two hundred.

POLICE: I was just, I was pulling a number out of the air there.

VG: No it was just random photos, you know, like random, you like, I'd do like little batches of them . . .

VG: I just used to change their nappy and take a photo, and then I'd text him saying 'oh, I've got three photos for you today', he's like 'oh', you know, 'lovely' and things like that and then I'd talk to him on MSN . . .

POLICE: So when did you take the first photograph?

VG: It wouldn't have been long after I started talking to him.

POLICE: So how many months ago?

VG: About five, four and a half, five?

POLICE: Are there any children you haven't taken a picture of?

VG: Yeah, I just do, just used to take like just, not all of them, no.

POLICE: Not all of them.

VG: No.

POLICE: So where were, where were the other staff when you were doing this?

VG: In with the other children.

POLICE: So you'd go off on your own?

VG: Yeah.

POLICE: Do you know who they are, their names?

VG: Um, no, it was just random.

POLICE: Boys, girls?

When you're changing them is there a door closing off giving you some privacy?

VG: There's doors, but I didn't shut the door.

POLICE: Why not?

VG: I wasn't doing it for like enjoyment or anything like that, I was just doing it for, just to take the photo.

POLICE: So you didn't get any sexual pleasure out of it yourself?

VG: No, not at all, no, I prefer men to be quite hon— I don't, it wasn't, it was just purely just to take a photo.

POLICE: And you were happy to give him the pictures?

VG: I wasn't, but, I knew it was wrong when I was doing it, when I was taking the photos, I knew it was wrong.

POLICE: What's wrong about it?

VG: Well, it's vile, it's not . . .

POLICE: Do you know it's against the law?

VG: Yes I do.

POLICE: As part of your job . . .

VG: Mmm.

POLICE: . . . have you done any child protection training?

VG: I did do years ago, yes, but we always do like refresher courses and things like that.

POLICE: Have you done the refresher courses?

VG: I don't think I have on that one, no.

POLICE: OK on which one?

VG: On the child protection.

POLICE: Just so I'm clear – you know it's against the law to take those type of pictures of children.

VG: We're not even supposed to take photos of the children's faces in the nursery without consent.

POLICE: Do you know that taking those pictures was abusing those children?

VG: Mmm.

POLICE: Those pictures are now distributed, they'll be all over, all over the world. Did you think about that when you took the pictures . . .

VG: No.

POLICE: Did it not occur to you that that might happen and that these children are now all over the world.

VG: I didn't think of that.

POLICE: I would say that you've been very honest with us . . .

VG: Yeah.

POLICE: . . . OK, and as we said when we were booking into custody about how your world's been blown apart to some extent hasn't it?

VG: Yeah, yeah.

POLICE: Do you think you might try and harm yourself?

VG: No, not at all.

POLICE: We'll go downstairs from here, but if when you're in the cell you think that you're having those thoughts or you're, I have to say it . . .

VG: No – I know you do, no.

POLICE: Cos what we don't want to do is anything happened to you.

VG: I'm too chicken, I'm sorry.

POLICE: Well your welfare's important to us.

VG: Yeah, I bet it is.

POLICE: The time is now 0217 hours and I'm going to stop the interview.

PART ONE

Beginnings

'There is always one moment in childhood when the
door opens and lets the future in.'

Graham Greene, *The Power and the Glory*

I

Plymouth is in many ways a city that looks as if it has seen better days. If one sits on a bench on Plymouth Hoe and gazes out past Smeaton's Tower with its distinctive red and white candy-stripes towards Plymouth Sound or Drake's Island, the spectacular coastal scenery hints at the city's grand maritime heritage, but a single glance towards the city centre is an all-too-obvious reminder that its glory days have faded into the past.

Plymouth city centre – largely rebuilt after the wartime bombing – has a neglected air, and once the chain stores and sandwich bars close at 5.30 or 6.00 a deadness pervades the wide, still streets. Those areas that do stay open after dark, like Mutley Plain, where students congregate, the bar-lined Union Street or the picturesque medieval Barbican, are often blighted by groups of binge-drinkers drawn by the two-for-one drinks offers or cut-price cocktails.

The city which once made history for its achievements in exploration and military endeavour is these days more likely to be in the headlines for less celebratory reasons. Most recently the Plymouth-raised teenage diving prodigy Tom Daley was reported to have been forced to move schools because he was being bullied by other kids jealous of his success. It is as if this is a city distrustful of outsiders, including those of its own who choose to spread their wings beyond its restrictive geographical parameters.

At times Plymouth can seem like two cities, divided between the indigenous population, often referred to as Janners, whose families have lived in the area for generations, and the temporary residents attached to either the university or the naval base. This deeply entrenched dichotomy can make it appear to be a city in conflict or in transition.

Some days it can be hard to believe that this city in search of an identity was once the jewel in Britain's maritime crown with a rich seafaring history going back to the Bronze Age. The story of Plymouth is inexorably linked to water as, in addition to the English Channel to the south, it is flanked by the River Plym to the east and the River Tamar to the west. Even as far back as the Bronze Age there was a settlement at Mount Batten. This settlement continued to grow as a trading post for the Roman Empire, until the more prosperous village of Sutton, sited on a small peninsula on the mouth of the River Plym and the ancestor of the current Plymouth, surpassed it.

The earliest record of cargo leaving Plymouth dates from 1211, and for the next two centuries trade through the port flourished, particularly during the Hundred Years War with France. Plymouth's importance both as a community and as a port accelerated during this period. In 1254 its town status was recognized by Royal Charter, and in 1439 Plymouth was the first town in England to be granted a Charter by Parliament. Trade with other English regions, the Baltic nations and Northern Europe expanded, while fortifications were built up to repel repeated French invasions.

During the next three centuries Plymouth established its reputation as a centre for voyage and discovery, as well as a strategic military base. In 1528 the first transatlantic trade began, and in 1588 Sir Francis Drake masterminded the defeat of the Spanish Armada. According to popular legend, he played bowls on Plymouth Hoe as the Armada sailed up the Channel. Drake was responsible also for the establishment of England's first colony, at Roanoke in Virginia, which kick-started the British Empire.

Perhaps the most famous expedition to leave Plymouth was that of the Pilgrim Fathers. Persecuted for their Puritan beliefs in eastern England, they set sail for the New World on board the *Mayflower* in 1620. After spending a few weeks in Provincetown at the tip of Cape Cod, they eventually landed in Plymouth Harbor and helped to establish a new Plymouth community in what would become the USA.

Further explorations that left from Plymouth included three voyages to the Southern Ocean and the Pacific made by James Cook, the first in 1768. He was the first explorer to set foot on what are now the Hawaiian Islands, where he died in 1779. In 1831 Charles Darwin left Plymouth for the Galapagos Islands, where he formulated his revolutionary theories of natural selection and the origin of species. Plymouth's military expansion began in earnest in 1670, when a citadel was built on the highest point in the town, the Hoe, meaning 'high ground'. In 1690 the first Royal Dockyard opened on the banks of the Tamar west of Plymouth. Further docks were built in 1727, 1762 and 1793, and a huge naval complex was later established, including the communities of Plymouth Dock and Stonehouse. The

Navy's role during the war against Napoleon's France was pivotal, and in 1812 a mile-long breakwater was laid to protect the fleet.

Throughout the nineteenth century the population and physical size of the towns increased dramatically. In 1824 Plymouth Dock was renamed Devonport, and in 1914 the three towns of Plymouth, Devonport and Stonehouse were united as the Borough of Plymouth, with Plymouth gaining city status fourteen years later.

But Plymouth's glittering history came crashing to an end in an almost hubristic, tower of Babel episode, bringing with it a sense of foreboding and hopelessness which many believe the city has still not recovered from to this day. In just seven terrifying nights during the spring of 1941, the centres of Plymouth and neighbouring Devonport were laid to ruin by Hitler's bombs. The devastating German air raids of the nights of 20 and 21 March and 21–3, 28 and 29 April have come to be termed the Plymouth Blitz.

The raids seem to have been triggered by a royal visit on 20 March. King George VI and Queen Elizabeth arrived in Plymouth by royal train at 10.30 a.m. and toured various parts of the city before departing at 5.45 p.m., by which time there were already rumours circulating around the Royal Air Force operational room at St Eval, in Cornwall, that 'Plymouth is due to catch a packet tonight.'

At just after 8.30 p.m. the alert was sounded and at 8.39 the attack started. Over the next four long hours, the centre of Plymouth was subjected to a sustained and terrifying bombing raid. By the time the raid ended at 12.20 a.m., in the early hours of 21 March, the middle of Plymouth was on fire.

At 8.50 p.m. the following night, Friday, 21 March, it started all over again, catching the still shell-shocked city by surprise. By the end of the night, only two buildings in the city centre were left standing – the National Westminster Bank in Bedford Street and the *Western Morning News* office, in Frankfort Street.

After that there followed a false calm as it appeared the bombers had achieved their objectives and moved on to a fresh target. But on Monday, 21 April, just as everyone was starting to breathe easier again, the now dreaded sound of the warning sirens rang out once again across the city's devastated streets. This time it was Devonport's turn to bear the brunt of the German air force's wrath. Through that night, and the two nights that followed, the people of Devonport huddled in underground shelters while the buildings around them collapsed and burned. Devonport Market was completely destroyed. That's not to say that other areas of the city escaped unscathed – seventy-two people were killed outright when an air raid shelter at Portland Square, opposite the City Museum, took a direct hit.

The reprieve that followed lasted just a few days. The following Monday, 28 April, the sky over Plymouth was once again lit up by enemy bombs. The Dockyard, St Budeaux, Camel's Head and Torpoint were all targeted, as was the Royal Naval Armament Depot. The next night it was the turn of Milehouse, Keyham and Saltash. By the time the worst of the raids was over in the early hours of

30 April, Plymouth was unrecognizable as the city it had been just a few weeks before.

Plymouth's children were badly affected by the Blitz. Issued with uncomfortable gas masks that made breathing impossible, they were forced to endure 'gas practice', where they'd stand in the back of a container lorry full of tear gas to make sure their masks were working properly. When the raids came, schools were destroyed overnight, leaving vast empty craters where playgrounds had so recently been. Night after night, they were shaken from their sleep and made to don their 'siren suits' over the top of their pyjamas and crawl into underground shelters, where they huddled together for warmth and comfort in the oppressive dampness, emerging at dawn terrified at what they might find.

It was left to the city's women, who stayed behind while the men were at war, to defend their children, their homes and their community. The windows of the houses had to be covered in strips of sticky paper to stop glass flying around if they were shattered. Each had also to be fitted with a blanket behind all the curtains to black out the light.

When the air raid sirens sounded, the women had to gather the children and the elderly and usher them quickly into the shelters, pulling blankets over the entrances. The younger women often acted as air raid wardens, risking their lives to search out incendiary bombs and using sand or water to put out the fires they had started. It was terrifying being out on the deserted streets, hearing the whistling of bombs falling through the air and feeling the ground beneath you shake as they landed. Occasionally, there'd be a blast so spectacular that the women would stop what they were doing and just stare in awe. When the Germans attacked Millbay Docks, provoking a display of gunfire and searchlights from the ships below, it was like the biggest firework display anyone had ever seen. Even the children were allowed out of the shelters to watch that one.

Vanessa George's grandmother, Kathleen – Kath – Budge, was typical of the women of Plymouth, trying hard to adapt to each new and often terrifying situation that the war foisted upon them. She was coping alone with one small child because her husband Bert was away serving with the merchant navy on an Atlantic convoy.

Like everyone else, Kath had to get used to living with food rationing, learning how to cook with powdered eggs and making two ounces of butter last a week. Also like every woman under forty, Kath was intrigued and slightly thrilled when thousands of Americans poured into Plymouth ahead of the D-Day landings. For a while the city was overrun with soldiers and sailors in uniform and there was a buzz about the place that was impossible to ignore – a welcome relief after the terror of the air raids and the relentless frugal drudgery of day-to-day war life. Then, overnight they were gone – the ships, men and machines all disappeared across the Channel, taking with them the jollity and excitement that their presence had generated and leaving behind in their wake piles of the hated Horlicks tablets and not a few broken hearts.

The end of the war brought conflicting emotions for many in Plymouth. On one hand they mourned loved ones they'd lost both in the bombings at home and on the frontline overseas. They also grieved for the loss of their city, where so many local landmarks had been reduced to rubble. But on the other hand what relief there was to be young and alive. As the men returned from the battlefields, women laid down their tools and their overalls and started once again to think about marriage and children: little wonder the years immediately following the war saw a huge jump in the birth rate – a statistical blip nicknamed the 'baby boom'.

Kath Budge was no exception. After her husband Bert's safe return from duty with the merchant navy, she soon got pregnant again and the family ended up being housed in a so-called prefabricated (known throughout Britain as 'prefab') house on a hastily erected estate on the edge of Plymouth called Lee Mills. Bert couldn't hide his slight disappointment when Kath gave birth to a second daughter but there was no time back in those days to rest on your laurels. Bert had a living to make and a family to support and those priorities overshadowed everything else. When daughters three and four were born in quick succession during the late 1940s, Bert just shrugged his shoulders.

On the whole Plymothians would be relieved to say goodbye to the 1940s, with its ponderous baggage of death and destruction, and welcome in a new decade. As the Budge family grew, all around them were other echoing signs of renewal and rebirth. Eventually a new city centre would emerge, with modern tower blocks and shops, and a massive programme of residential rebuilding.

The Budges eventually moved from their post-war

prefabricated home on the Lee Mills housing estate to a brand-new three-bedroomed council house in Greystokes Road, in the Eggbuckland area of Plymouth. Like so many of the newly created housing complexes in Plymouth back then, it had been the site of a farm until urban planners decided to make it part of the city's expansion plans to house tens of thousands of families displaced by Hitler's bombing raids ten years earlier.

Eggbuckland – once a sleepy semi-rural village – found itself at the centre of an ambitious new housing regeneration scheme. Vast new housing estates were planned, stretching the boundaries of Plymouth to breaking point. The Budge girls were growing up in an era alive with new possibilities, and yet somehow, as the optimistic fifties faded out into the more cynical sixties, these possibilities never really materialized. As its fields were tarmacked and cemented over to make space for its new influx of residents, Eggbuckland lost its old rural identity without ever really finding anything to go in its place. But for the families who moved into the new estates and, like the Budges, became part of the evolving community, it was a decent enough place to bring up children and lay down roots.

The estate where the Budges lived was eventually called Eggbuckland Farm and just across the valley the Deer Park estate was also constructed, so that in the space of a few years hundreds of acres of farmland were transformed into housing estates. A main road was even built right through the middle of the two estates.

Kath, Bert and their four daughters were soon well-known in Greystokes Road. By this time Bert worked in the nearby shipyard, although he would eventually retire at a relatively young age owing to health problems.

The houses in Greystokes Road were much sought after because they were new, had huge, long gardens and cost tenants a very modest one guinea a week in rent. As one resident who still lives on the estate recently explained: 'This was a prime location for council tenants. The houses were brand new and relatively luxurious compared to what we had all been used to straight after the war.'

All four of Kath and Bert's daughters – June, Valerie, Janet and Sylvia – had been born before the family took up residence at number 57, Greystokes Road. All the girls went to the local Eggbuckland schools and they soon became familiar faces in the community.

Sylvia, the youngest – who'd been born on 17 June 1948 – always had a twinkle in her eye, according to neighbours. 'She was a lovely little girl, always smiling and laughing and she definitely seemed the most gregarious of all the girls,' said one Greystokes Road resident many years later.

Sylvia and her sisters spent most of their time playing in the family's hundred-foot-long back garden, although they were sometimes seen hopping and skipping out on the quiet road in front of the house. 'Sylvia was always humming and singing to herself,' added the neighbour. 'She was such a happy little girl.'

And all around Greystokes Road, more and more new houses were constructed as part of the city's post-war effort to create homes for all those displaced families. Street after street was built around Greystokes until the Eggbuckland Farm estate had become virtually a self-contained community with its own row of shops and businesses, including a post office, a fruit and veg shop, a hairdresser's and a butcher.

However, Bert Budge was not one of the most popular residents of Greystokes Road. According to one neighbour: 'Bert used to report people for not having tax on their cars and many of us wondered why he didn't just mind his own business.'

His daughter Janet's husband, Barry Medway, thought: 'Bert Budge was very straitlaced. He was also always saying he was ill, like a hypochondriac, I suppose. He wasn't the easiest man in the world to get on with.'

Another Greystokes Road resident was even more blunt about Bert. 'He was the neighbour from hell who never seemed capable of minding his own business but his wife Kath was very different. She was a happy, loud person although she certainly didn't suffer fools gladly.'

Bert Budge was extremely proud of his gleaming, spotless, black Ford Prefect car, which he always parked right outside number 57. 'He'd go completely potty if anyone else was parked in his space,' said one neighbour. 'And he used to spend hours every Sunday proudly cleaning that car. I think it was his way of escaping all those women in his household.'

But despite his long, hard hours working down at the shipyard, Bert did find time to play an organ at various local pubs, although by all accounts he wasn't a particularly skilful musician. 'He didn't get paid anything and a lot of regulars would roll their eyes when Bert walked in and started playing but at least he was fearless about it. I don't think he cared what anyone else thought.'

When the youngest daughter, Sylvia, showed an interest in music, Bert allowed her to accompany him to the pub during the day at weekends, although she'd often have to sit outside while he played the organ inside because children were not allowed in pubs back in those days. Sylvia was captivated by the whole idea of playing music for people and being appreciated by an audience. As one relative later explained: 'Sylvia was a natural performer and her eyes would sparkle up with excitement just to be allowed to go with her dad to watch him play.' Bert was a regular at a number of local pubs near his home but he wasn't a heavy drinker by anyone's standards.

Back at number 57, Greystokes Road, the Budge family seemed relatively happy and content with their lives. The house was very neat and tidy, so much so that neither Kath nor Bert would allow the girls to have a pet dog or cat. There were few domestic dramas, although Sylvia and her sisters did seem a little overweight. But there was nothing particularly unusual about that and everyone in the family put that down to Kath's obsession with making sure her girls were well-fed. 'Sylvia looked a lot like her mum and they were both a little on the heavy side but it was nothing out of the ordinary,' one relative said many years later.

The only memorable thing about the four Budge sisters was that they seemed so well-behaved all the time. 'It was almost unnatural the way they were so polite and some of us did wonder if they were a little timid and scared because of the way old Bert treated them but, to be fair, no one ever saw him hitting them or anything like that,' said a neighbour.

Eventually the three eldest girls moved out of number 57, leaving Sylvia, who'd turned into a typical mid-1960s teenager with 'a sharp bob and a quick wit'. One neighbour described how 'Sylvia was different from the other girls. She had this rebellious look of defiance in her eyes. I wouldn't say she was rebellious but she was a lot more outgoing than the rest of the family.' And much to Bert Budge's irritation, a lot of local boys were starting to take an interest in the pretty teenager.

'One of Sylvia's first serious boyfriends was a boy called Doug, who had to drive her father Bert to the doctor's loads of times in his Ford Anglia because Bert was always moaning about being ill,' recalled one relative. 'Of course, Bert was putting it all on in order to keep an eye on Sylvia and this boy Doug.'

But then Sylvia was the apple of Bert's eye. 'They shared an enthusiasm for music and Bert was undoubtedly softer on Sylvia than the other girls because she was the baby of the family,' added the relative.

But Bert Budge knew that his daughter Sylvia's passion for music – which he had encouraged since she was young – would send her on many adventures, some of which he would rather not know about. Bert seemed to accept that his headstrong youngest daughter had a will of her own and there was nothing he could do to change that.

Kath Budge had always loved cooking and looking after all her beloved daughters and she admitted to friends that she dearly missed the three eldest when they moved away. But she would eventually miss them in an even more tragic way.

Kath's youngest daughter was by this time working in a shop in the daytime and had developed her love of music to such an extent that she'd begun singing with a pub group in Plymouth called the Raymond Trio. Their drummer was a slender, dark-haired man, with a soft voice and quiet nature, called Roger Marks. As Roger explained many years later: 'Sylvia caught my eye the first time I saw her and then Bert Putt, our band leader, said playfully to me that it was her birthday that day and I should give her a special kiss and I thought I'll do better than that. I fancied her something rotten.'

Roger Marks's dad Stan was a retired policeman who by this time owned and ran his own farm. Roger – one of three brothers and two sisters – still lived at home with Stan and his mother Winnie. Roger's day job was in a local shipping yard so he understood and appreciated how tricky it was to make a proper living from music. He also knew it was high time he left home.

It was 1969, and while flower power might have been booming at the time, Roger Marks and Sylvia Budge were far from hippies. Roger's hair was longish but he and his fellow band members favoured bow-ties and smart jackets with velvet lapels when they performed and Sylvia – with her long, flowing, dark hair – tended to wear smock-type dresses that hid her weight. However, those who encountered the pair back in the later 1960s say they made a strikingly attractive couple. 'We were the opposite of hippies,' recalled Roger. 'I was not interested in drugs. Drink was my only weakness.' As 'musicians' in the relatively small artists' community of Plymouth at that time, people like Roger and Sylvia were greatly admired for 'doing their own thing'.

A few weeks after starting to play with the Raymond Trio, Sylvia accepted Roger's invitation to visit him at his parents' farm just outside Plymouth for lunch. A typically deadpan Roger remarked: 'One thing led to another and we ended up having sex in one of the barns. It just sort of happened but neither of us took it to mean we were starting a proper relationship. We just fancied doing it so we did. End of story.'

Well, it would have been the end of this entire story except for one problem: Sylvia got pregnant. As Roger put it: 'I was stunned.' At first he refused to accept that he was the father. 'I mean I didn't know if I was the only bloke she'd even been with at that time. I got so freaked out I decided to lie low for a while and avoid her.'

In fact Roger had only found out about the pregnancy when Sylvia's father Bert called up to tell him. 'He wasn't happy and demanded that I marry Sylvia.' But instead Roger ran away from his responsibilities. 'Typical me, I am afraid. For a while I just hoped she'd go away and leave me alone.'

But Sylvia began bombarding Roger with phone calls, and when she heard nothing back from him, she went back to the farm where her baby had been conceived and started banging on the front door for him to come out. When neither Roger nor his parents answered, Sylvia grabbed a broom and started smashing in all the front windows of the main building. By the time she had finished she'd caused hundreds of pounds' worth of damage. 'She was very emotional because she was pregnant and she thought I wasn't going to marry her and this was her way of letting me know she was angry,' explained Roger. 'My parents thought she was a complete nutter but they told me I had to deal with her so I decided to do the right thing and buy a house and marry her.'

So, six months after that 'quick shag in a barn', as Roger describes it, the couple got married in a local register office and Roger bought a house in Crozier Road, Plymouth, for £2,400 on a mortgage. He put it like this: 'She was six months pregnant when we married. My parents didn't pressure me. I asked her again if it was my child and she insisted it was so I did the right thing.'

Sylvia refused to move in with Roger until she had the baby but as he now recalls: 'At least I managed to finally move out from my parents' home, which was a relief.'

Not surprisingly – as Sylvia would later tell a friend – cracks quickly began to appear in the couple's relationship. 'Sylvia soon noticed that Roger had a tendency to drink himself into a bit of a stupor and sometimes he would disappear for days,' said one old friend.

However, Sylvia still believed there was a genuine connection between them through their love of music and their determination to eventually make a full-time living from it. Roger remembered: 'I liked a drink. My favourite tipple was a pint of bitter back in those days. Sylvia preferred sweet Martini but neither of us went anywhere near drugs.' In fact, Sylvia's father Bert had made it clear that drugs were the Devil's candy.

Sylvia had no day job at the time so she spent most of

the rest of her pregnancy staying at her parents' home in Greystokes Road. Meanwhile Roger was working at the nearby shipyard and the couple would, somewhat bizarrely, meet some evenings when they played with the Raymond Trio together at various pubs and clubs around Plymouth. But then Sylvia stunned Roger by joining another group called the George Howard Sound. As Roger Marks later described: 'The Trio was more like a big-band style. The George Howard Sound was more ballady and did a lot of cover versions of famous songs. But Sylvia had a good, interesting voice and she reckoned she was too good for the Trio. If the *X Factor* was on the telly back then she would have been on it. She wanted fame.'

Meanwhile, back at home, the couple saw even less of each other. 'I thought it was odd that she would leave the trio but the Sound were a much bigger band and Sylvia was very ambitious in that sense and she said she preferred their music. It made me feel a bit insecure because I ended up spending a lot of time at home on my own while she was always out and about or at her parents' house.'

It was an exhausting existence and today Roger openly admits their relationship was a recipe for disaster: 'I was working round the clock to pay the mortgage and look after Sylvia and she wasn't even staying with me in the house. It wasn't much fun.'

Roger reflected: 'Looking back on it, having sex with Sylvia had been just a one-off. I was horrified she'd got pregnant. I knew Sylvia was trouble and I was still unsure whether I was the father of the child but I still thought to myself, "What the hell? I might as well try and make a go of it." I wanted to do the honourable thing. Sylvia was a dreadful fantasist. She got off on lying and winding things up. It seems like Vanessa is similar to that today. She must have got it from her mother. Sylvia could be a very difficult person but in some weird way I was in love with her.'

But he added: 'The trouble is, the moment I married Sylvia I thought, "Shit. What have I done? I shouldn't be here."'

Neither Roger nor Sylvia had given any proper consideration to the long-term prospects of their relationship. 'Getting her pregnant was in many ways the beginning of the end,' said Roger Marks.

2

Roger Marks's relationship with his new young pregnant wife Sylvia was already strained when he got 'completely plastered' the night before their child was born after the couple had yet another massive row. As a result, he didn't even know which hospital Sylvia had gone to when she went into labour. 'I remember it was snowing that morning and the exhaust on my car had gone and I was racing around from hospital to hospital trying to find out where Sylvia was.'

Roger eventually found his wife at Plymouth's Freedom Fields Hospital, but he got there too late for the birth of their baby daughter, Vanessa Sylvia Marks, on 30 March 1970.

Roger vividly recalled: 'I remember walking in and there she was already breastfeeding the child. I was stunned to have missed the birth, but then I started looking more closely at that baby's features and I knew then that there was no way she was my child.'

Within half an hour of arriving at the hospital, Roger Marks confronted his exhausted wife. 'She's not mine,' he told Sylvia. She responded with a look he later described as being 'as hard as nails'. Then she told her husband: 'Of course she is.' As Roger remembered: 'That was it. She wouldn't speak about it any more after that. Sylvia had a hardness and a coldness to her. I've seen it in Vanessa since her arrest. I don't know where it comes from but it's not very nice.'

So Sylvia and Roger already had a volatile relationship, which was further strained by the arrival of a baby on the scene. A few months before giving birth, Sylvia had joined the George Howard Sound. Roger had remained with the Raymond Trio so by the time Vanessa was born they were leading virtually separate lives. The George Howard Sound were so well regarded they had a high-profile 'spot' at the Plymouth Holiday Inn every Saturday night. Roger Marks had not been considered a good enough drummer to join them. This caused even more tension between the parents of the newly born Vanessa.

Soon flyers featuring the George Howard Sound were appearing all over Plymouth and the band's leader, George Farley, had special cards printed up which showed a photo of the group playing, featuring Sylvia in a long, flowing white dress. Below the photo was written: 'Presenting The George Howard Sound. Music to suit all occasions. Hotels, clubs, private functions, engagement parties and wedding receptions. Keep Music Live.'

George Farley became a father figure to Sylvia, who by all accounts regularly poured all her troubles out to the band leader. Even Roger Marks admits today: 'Farley looked after Sylvia and they were good friends but definitely not lovers.'

Back at home, Roger found himself spending more and more evenings baby-sitting Vanessa while his pretty young wife was out singing at different venues around the Plymouth area. 'I was working hard in the day while Sylvia was at home and then we'd reverse roles in the evening. It wasn't exactly the recipe for a good marriage.'

He also heard rumours about Sylvia and 'other men', including one piece of very damaging gossip about how Sylvia had a one-night stand with a then famous rock star called Screaming Lord Sutch after he performed a concert in Plymouth.

And every time there was a row at home, Roger made a point of bringing up the subject of who Vanessa's real father actually was. 'I was utterly convinced she wasn't mine and every time I confronted Sylvia we got nastier about it. She'd go mental and then I would storm off to the pub to get away from her temper tantrums. Then I'd come back and we'd start all over again.'

Today Roger Marks says he would be willing to take a DNA test to prove he is *not* Vanessa George's father. 'I want to end the connection once and for all because I just will never believe she is my child. It's just not possible. I look at her today and see this huge hulk of a woman and yet I am short, slight and very thin. It just doesn't make sense.' He added: 'I am convinced she is not my child.'

Sylvia was getting increasingly fed up with Roger Marks's heavy drinking, though. One time she marched into the pub where he'd been all evening and slapped down a plate of food in front of him. Roger recalled: 'It was on a tray with a bottle of sauce and she just said, "You fuckin' live here so you might as well eat here." I just said, "Thanks" and carried on drinking.'

Then about eighteen months after Vanessa was born, Sylvia got pregnant again. Roger Marks takes up the story:

'I was actually delighted because this time I was convinced the baby was mine and it sort of made me feel that perhaps we had a chance to mend our marriage. It seemed to make up for the way I'd been having to pretend Vanessa had been mine for so long.'

Then Sylvia hit Roger with a bombshell just moments after revealing she was pregnant. 'I'm going to have an abortion,' she told her husband. 'I was distraught,' said Roger. 'I pleaded with her not to do it but she went ahead and did it. That was probably when I knew for sure we wouldn't last much longer. She had that abortion to spite me.'

After that incident, Roger Marks spent more and more time at the pub and Sylvia was out most evenings singing with the George Howard Sound. Caught in the middle of all this domestic chaos was little Vanessa. Roger remembered that 'The neighbours were usually roped in to do the baby-sitting. I don't think we were hardly ever together in the same room with Vanessa. We certainly never went on one holiday throughout her early childhood.'

He added: 'I kept thinking it would get better one day but it never did. We were like two strangers who'd been thrown together by one bit of sex in a barn. We avoided each other and that's how we kept going. Sometimes we'd cross on the stairs at home and barely acknowledge each other.'

And nights were punctuated by a lot of crying from baby Vanessa. 'She cried a lot and every time I looked at her in Sylvia's arms I knew she wasn't my baby. She didn't look anything like me and she was big and I didn't feel any real connection to her.'

So, as Sylvia began getting more and more 'gigs' with

the band, her husband Roger found himself being left behind, in every sense of the word. He had recently left his job as a shipwright and taken a new daytime position as a mill operator. He then moved on to work at a company called English China Clay.

Sylvia was by this time performing at pubs and clubs in and around Plymouth up to five nights a week. Occasionally, Roger got work with the Raymond Trio as a drummer and little Vanessa continued to be looked after by friends or baby-sitters.

When Vanessa was about three years old, Roger and Sylvia were involved in a serious car crash which almost ended Sylvia's singing career. She suffered serious facial wounds from the windscreen of their car when another vehicle hit them coming in the opposite direction. As Roger later recalled: 'Singing was the most important thing in Sylvia's life so when her face was cut and scarred she was very upset because she couldn't do any singing for months after the accident.'

Then one day, when Vanessa was about four, Roger Marks's parents called him up on the phone to tell him they had 'bumped into' Sylvia at a pub where his retired policeman father was delivering eggs and chickens. Roger explained: 'Sylvia was leaving the living quarters at the back of the pub. She was walking down the stairs one dinner-time and my dad asked her what she was doing and she just walked straight past him and ignored him. Well, it was obvious that Sylvia was having an affair with that publican. He was an arrogant bastard so it all made sense to me when they told me.'

Yet another row ensued when Sylvia got home later that same day. 'I'd been in all day and night looking after Vanessa while she'd slept with another bloke. It was completely out of order. But when I confronted her she just said, "I wasn't there."' Not surprisingly, Roger says he brought up the subject 'over and over again but she always denied it'.

But tensions inside the house in Crozier Road were building all the time and Roger Marks insists it was his wife – not him – who was prone to violence. 'She would come at me with her fists flying and I'd just try to walk away but it wasn't easy.' But despite all this he concedes that his ex-wife 'tried her hardest to be a good mother. She really did, although she found it hard.'

According to Marks, who now lives in Plympton, near Plymouth, his alleged daughter Vanessa had a troubled early childhood because he and Sylvia rowed constantly. It's difficult to know what sort of effect this might have had on the little girl, but he openly admits that the tensions in the house regularly went past boiling point. One relative recalled: 'Vanessa must have seen a lot of nasty stuff between her parents in those early years of her childhood. She was a chatty little child with a large round face and as I recall she couldn't stop yapping all the time. I guess that was her way of dealing with what she saw.'

And Sylvia's determination to make it as a singer did not help. She insisted on continuing to tour the pubs and clubs with the George Howard Sound and often she would not get home until the early hours. 'The trouble was that Roger did nothing around the house so Sylvia would come home and find the place looking like a tip and then have to do all the housework before snatching a few hours' sleep and then getting up to go to her day job,' explained a family friend.

Then one day Roger arrived back from work at the house in Crozier Road to be greeted by Sylvia and a woman neighbour. 'The neighbour was there as a witness because Sylvia said she wanted a divorce and she wanted me out of the house there and then. I was stunned. I packed one bag and went to my parents' farm. I knew it was the end and I was relieved in a sense, even though I loved Sylvia despite all the problems. But I guess we were doomed from the start.'

Within weeks, Roger had agreed to give Sylvia and Vanessa the house in Crozier Road. 'She said if I gave it to her outright then she wouldn't ask for maintenance. So like a fool I agreed and then she went to court to get me to pay maintenance anyway. But I have to take responsibility. The marriage broke up mainly because of my drinking and womanizing.'

Despite later claims to the contrary, Roger Marks fulfilled his parental duties by paying maintenance every month to Sylvia. He even recalled having Vanessa to stay at his parents' farm, where he had moved back after the split. 'Vanessa was very precocious and seemed to be a right know-all about everything but she got that from her mother.'

But what Vanessa then said has always grated with Roger Marks. 'She said to me, "We got that nice house off you", which really upset me because then it felt like I'd been tricked by Sylvia after she told me to leave the house.'

Roger Marks later tried to put a brave face on the end of his marriage: 'We would never have stayed together for life. I would have killed her in the end, even though I am not a violent person.'

Today, he can only recall his daughter as 'intelligent' and 'quite precocious'. He remembers she loved being the centre of attention and would turn on an act to ensure she was centre-stage. 'Vanessa was a strange child,' Roger says. 'She was bright as a button and very clever. She was quite precocious; a bit of a show-off and confident and probably mature beyond her years.' He is convinced his former wife ensured that he rarely saw Vanessa again by poisoning her against him.

It seemed that young Vanessa dealt with the 'confusion' and unhappiness of her parents' divorce by creating a 'happy bubble' to retreat into to avoid the reality of what was happening around her. It had worked well when her parents were constantly rowing and later in life she would use it in order to achieve her self-centred objectives for happiness.

Following the divorce, Vanessa and her mother Sylvia continued living at number 1, Crozier Road. Sylvia was known locally for driving around Plymouth in a collection of old bangers because she could barely afford the cost of motoring. Crozier Road was a quiet, very short street within walking distance of all the main shops and at least it meant that Sylvia wouldn't face a long journey back late at night from her singing appearances with the George Howard Sound because she was determined not to quit music. She told one relative it was the most important thing in her life. Sylvia didn't even mention Vanessa in the same breath. The relative explained: 'Music was Sylvia's lifeblood. Without it, she just felt as ordinary as the next person but when she was on stage she became an important person, almost famous in a sense, and she loved that feeling.'

Vanessa didn't seem, at least outwardly, to have been so badly affected by her parents' split-up. She loved going to school and was by this time attending the Lipson Vale primary, where she was bubbly and outgoing and very bossy towards many of the other children, not to mention the teachers. One family friend later recalled: 'Vanessa had a sparkle to her which I suppose she got from her mother. She was confident and very large for her age and a lot of the other children looked up to her.'

Her teachers later recalled that Vanessa seemed almost scarily grown-up for her years. 'She was very capable of doing things for herself,' said one of them.

With Sylvia out working all day and then often singing at night, it was hardly surprising that Vanessa had learned to look after herself so early on. From the time of her parents' break-up she'd become virtually a latch-key kid, letting herself into the house in Crozier Road most after-noons after school. One neighbour recalled: 'Vanessa looked about eleven when she was seven or eight so it didn't seem so surprising that she would let herself into the house after school and make herself tea and stuff like that until her mother got home from work.'

But Sylvia would often go straight from her latest day job selling promotional items in supermarkets to meet the other members of the group for a gig – leaving her young daughter to fend entirely for herself.

But not even easy-going Sylvia felt she could get away with leaving Vanessa at night on her own so some local 'friends' were recruited as 'baby-sitters'. As one former neighbour in Crozier Road later explained: 'They weren't what you'd normally call baby-sitters. A lot of them were middle-aged men who Sylvia seemed to know from her appearances as a singer.' In fact, some of those so-called 'baby-sitters' were part-time lodgers whom Sylvia sublet rooms to in the three-bedroomed house in order to make ends meet.

One neighbour summed up Sylvia thus: 'She was a lovely person but she was incredibly selfish. It wasn't really neglect but she always put herself ahead of Vanessa and would never do anything for anybody else. It was always all about Sylvia. But she did love Vanessa, though. But we always wondered how she could leave that child on her own or with baby-sitters and not worry about it. I would never have left my children like that but that was Sylvia for you.'

Sylvia's three elder sisters seemed a lot more settled and sensible than her. Their mother Kath was immensely proud of all her 'girls', so when her eldest daughter, June, was diagnosed with cancer it came as a complete shock. June – then in her early forties – had married and moved to Swindon, in Wiltshire, many years earlier. She died some months later and Kath was badly shaken by the premature death of her daughter at such a young age. Friends and relatives put it all down to bad luck and never once did doctors think back then that deadly cancer genes might be lying dormant in all the female members of the family. 'It

just wasn't something that you talked about back then,'
explained one family friend. 'June's death was tragic but
you just got on with your life after something like that
happened. There was no time or inclination to sit around
and discuss what it all meant.'

Some old neighbours from Greystokes Road, where the
Budge girls had grown up, attended June's funeral and one
later recalled: 'When Kath and Bert moved away we didn't
expect to see much more of them and we certainly didn't
think we'd end up meeting them again at the funeral of
one of their own daughters. It was a very sad affair and
Kath was obviously shattered by losing her daughter.'

When Vanessa was twelve she went to the now demolished
Burleigh secondary school, in nearby Crownhill. By this
time she looked at least fifteen and boys in the area were
starting to take an interest in her. She was large and quite
masculine-looking thanks in part to her short hairstyle. But
she still always had a smile on her face and was quick to
throw in a cheeky, flirtatious remark that made some of
them believe she might be 'up for a laugh'.

One former neighbour in Crozier Road thought that
'Vanessa seemed very fearless. She'd learned to grow up
fast and she was confident in the company of adults because she was so used to having them in the house she
shared with her mum.'

Vanessa's uncle, Barry Medway – married to Sylvia's
sister, Janet – still smiled when he recalled how the teenager
and three of her aunts did the hokey-cokey at a family
Christmas party at her Aunt Valerie's home in St Jude.

Proudly studying a photo he had taken of them all together, he said: 'They were all happy-go-lucky people and Vanessa looked the happiest of all of them in that photo.'

Vanessa's relatives believe that this was probably the happiest period of her childhood. One of them later remembered that 'Vanessa and Sylvia were very close and she was always very happy to see us all at family gatherings like at Christmas. I think Vanessa yearned to be part of a big family in a sense and she was certainly not shy at these sorts of events. In fact she always seemed to be positively glowing.'

But another recalled that Vanessa's bluntness could sometimes be very alarming. 'I remember hearing her talking about the boys at her school and she was very coarse about them. It was obvious she hadn't had much guidance on how to deal with children of her own age, which was a shame because she seemed very grown-up and capable in other ways.'

And Vanessa's grandparents, Kath and Bert Budge, were fairly old-fashioned, which didn't help either. Vanessa's Uncle Barry admitted he never enjoyed a particularly close relationship with his in-laws. 'Kath was all right but I never really got on with her very well. The trouble was that, as a couple, she and Bert would always be talking across each other and would interrupt each other so you never got anywhere with them. I used to give up talking in the end and just leave them to it.'

However, Barry visited Kath and Bert's house in Wellington Street, where they now lived, for most family birthday and Christmas parties so he got to know Vanessa reasonably well and still proudly talks about those far-off days when he looks back at his family snapshots from that period. 'Look, we were a normal family with all the usual ups and downs but you can tell from these photos that we were close enough to enjoy each other's company and my wife Janet and her sisters had a very close bond to each other, despite the early death of June.'

Meanwhile Sylvia had met and fallen in love with a married man who was well-known in the community. He recently spoke to this author about his affair with her on condition he was not identified. 'Sylvia was a wonderful free spirit, a breath of fresh air, but her life was chaos. I fell in love with her. She wanted me to leave my wife but after an intense affair that lasted nearly three years I had to end it because of my marriage. I knew it would never work properly with Sylvia, although I miss her every day of my life.'

Sylvia's secret married lover says he was aware of 'problems' with baby-sitters but refused to be drawn on exactly what those 'problems' were. 'Vanessa didn't get much attention as a child and I felt sorry for her but I tried not to get too involved with that side of things. My relationship with Sylvia was complicated enough as it was.'

But around this time – in 1983 – neighbours back in Crozier Road began noticing a change in Vanessa's character. She was thirteen years old by this time. One relative recalled: 'She was still happy and smiling on the outside but she seemed very tense underneath it and we all wondered what was happening to her.'

Some of the neighbours who lived near the small double-fronted house in Crozier Road where Sylvia and Vanessa lived got to know them well. They all had young families and their young children would play together. One neighbour explained: 'We took pity on Vanessa in many ways. She seemed such a lonely child. Sylvia was struggling to make ends meet but most nights she would either leave Vanessa home alone while she was out singing with that band or she would get one of her friends – often men – to baby-sit while she was out into the early hours of the morning.'

It was during this period that friends and relatives believe something happened to young Vanessa, which would possibly influence her in later life in a most disturbing way. According to one friend of her mother's: 'There were incidents with baby-sitters. Vanessa was abused by at least one of them who looked after her while Sylvia was out singing with her band. We only heard about it later but some of the things that happened to Vanessa were truly horrendous. That poor child must have been scarred for life.'

Vanessa's Uncle Barry also believed 'There may have been a problem with some of the baby-sitters who looked after Vanessa and it involved them abusing her. Vanessa was always being left on her own while Sylvia went out to sing with her group. There were many nights when she was looked after by virtual strangers when she was a child. Something nasty may have happened to her. But no one likes to talk about it.'

Barry refused to be drawn into any more detail but emphasized that nothing could excuse his niece's appalling catalogue of later crimes. 'But it is important to know the full story of her childhood because it wasn't easy for her,' he said. 'Although that doesn't make what she did any less shocking.'

He also revealed that following Sylvia's split from Vanessa's father, Roger Marks, she had quite a number of boyfriends, including at least one who lived with her and Vanessa at their home in Crozier Road. 'Oh yes. He lived there for quite some time so I suppose that must have been hard for Vanessa to deal with as well.' He continued: 'We used to go and see Sylvia quite a bit when she lived in Crozier Road and she was always getting baby-sitters in to look after Vanessa. We were worried about what might be happening. Sometimes she even left Vanessa on her own.'

Roger Marks spoke of one strange neighbour called 'Charlie' who often baby-sat Vanessa: 'I remember him and he was a bit weird but I wasn't involved by that stage so who Sylvia chose to baby-sit Vanessa was up to her. I wouldn't be surprised if Vanessa was abused. Nothing about her life would surprise me now. It was chaotic.'

Another neighbour of Sylvia's in Crozier Road talked to this author on condition she remained anonymous. 'There were big problems with baby-sitters. I think something awful happened with Vanessa and it is something that needs to come out because it does tell us so much about how Vanessa developed as a person. I knew Sylvia very well. She was a charming, bubbly personality but her parenting skills left a lot to be desired.'

The same neighbour also confirmed that the elderly male neighbour called 'Charlie' often baby-sat Vanessa and there were a lot of other neighbours who wondered why Sylvia would leave a single old man in charge of a young girl. 'It just didn't seem right. This man was a very lonely fellow and we were surprised when he started baby-sitting Vanessa. That man died long ago but he was a very strange individual.'

But there was an even bigger bombshell about to rock young Vanessa's life.

3

In late 1984 – when Vanessa was just fourteen years old – one of Sylvia's old neighbours from when she was growing up in Greystokes Road bumped into Sylvia when she was working as a singer. He takes up the story: 'We walked into the Beacon Park Social Club and there was Sylvia singing with a band. She was really good and had the most fantastic voice. She specialized in ballads and had a cracking voice.'

During a break in her performance, Sylvia made a point of seeking out her old neighbour for a chat. After a few minutes of small talk, Sylvia dropped a bombshell with typical, disarming honesty: 'I've got cancer.'

The former neighbour recalled: 'She just threw it in the conversation as if it was as normal as discussing the weather. We were stunned but I have to hand it to her for not looking for sympathy. She was just being very honest. That was typical of Sylvia.'

Moments later, Sylvia went back up on the small stage in the social club and started singing with the George Howard Sound. As her old neighbour later said: 'She looked so well back then it was very shocking to think she was dying. She just didn't look like she had cancer.'

Another relative remembered: 'It was so tragic. Just before her cancer had been diagnosed, Sylvia told us all she had fallen in love with this new man, who had a high-powered job with the local Plymouth City Council and that she was hoping this was "the one" who might give Sylvia the love and attention she craved but never seemed to find after splitting with Roger Marks.'

But all this obviously came crashing down after Sylvia was told she had the same illness as the one which had already ended the life of her eldest sister. Only in her mid-teens, Vanessa found it hard to absorb the seriousness of her mother's illness at first. But within months of that appearance in the Beacon Park Social Club, Sylvia Marks was in a wheelchair in a hospice in Plymouth having been told by doctors she had weeks to live. It was only then that the full impact of what had happened must have sunk in with the teenager. Up until then, Sylvia had tried to go about her work and life as if she was perfectly healthy, even though she had been undergoing treatment for months before she had to go into the hospice. One family friend later recalled: 'It hit Vanessa really badly. She was about to have to face the world and all its obstacles alone. That's very tough for a child, especially with no father around.'

Her Uncle Barry never forgot the difficult period after Sylvia began suffering from cancer because it mirrored his own later life. 'My wife and I went to see Sylvia in the hospice here in Plymouth which has since been knocked down. That's where she died. She was in there for the last few weeks of her life and it was a very difficult time.'

Another relative later recalled having Vanessa to stay at her home for a couple of days while her mother lay dying in the hospice. 'It was very disturbing because Vanessa just stopped speaking. She'd been a happy-go-lucky child before that but she'd sit on her own in the back garden just rocking back and forth, deep in thought and unable to play with the other children. One time I found her at the end of the garden hiding behind a tree refusing to come for dinner when it was being called. She had a glaze of moisture across her eyes but when I asked her if she was all right she just put on a plastic smile and said, "Yes." And when I tried to give her a cuddle she brushed me away very coldly. She just didn't seem able to deal with anyone being close to her.'

Thrown into each other's company, Sylvia and Vanessa had formed a very close mother and daughter bond after Roger Marks had left home more than seven years earlier. Now the young Vanessa was going to have to face life alone. Her school work was soon deteriorating even though she refused point-blank to admit she was feeling deeply affected by her mother's illness.

Yet throughout this period not one of her mother's relatives contacted Roger Marks to tell him that his ex-wife was dying. Roger explained: 'I only found out when my sister bumped into Sylvia in the street in Plymouth and she said she had cancer and was about to go into a hospice.'

Roger Marks – despite all the bitterness surrounding their divorce – was stunned and upset when he heard the news and immediately began a search of the city's hospitals in a bid to locate Sylvia. 'I eventually found her in St Luke's and I went to see her. She put on a brave face but I could see she was just days from dying. It was very heart-breaking.'

Sylvia eventually died at the St Luke's Hospice on 5 May 1985 at the age of just thirty-six, an event which Vanessa's alleged father Roger later conceded would have 'shattered Vanessa's world'.

The funeral service for Sylvia was held the following Friday, 10 May, at the Efford Crematorium. But when Roger Marks told the family he would like to attend, George Farley – leader of the George Howard Sound – rang Roger up and told him he would not be welcome at the service. 'He just said, "I don't want you there" so I took the hint and stayed away. Looking back on it I should have taken no notice of them,' recalled Roger.

Many years later one of George Farley's oldest friends explained the background to his relationship with Sylvia. 'George was always very worried about Sylvia. He knew what she had been through by being married to Roger and he felt that Roger shouldn't be at the funeral because it would so upset Sylvia's family as well as her friends in the George Howard Sound. George was a good man who worked hard in the day as a caretaker to be able to afford to run the group in the evenings, but I remember he was heartbroken by Sylvia's death. The group carried on but it was never the same after she died.'

There were two death notices in the local paper regarding Sylvia which seemed to sum up the two completely separate lives she led. One was from her family and included a simple prayer: 'God bless and keep you in His care.'

The other death notice was placed by members of the George Howard Sound and it said: 'The golden voice of the George Howard Sound passed away after a long illness very bravely borne. She will be missed by all the band and the very many people to whom she gave so much pleasure with her singing.' It was signed: 'From George, Jack, Bunny, Lesley and Corrina.'

A few days later an article about Sylvia's death appeared in the local paper. It was headlined 'SINGER'S DEATH AT 36' and talked about Sylvia's 'unusual and adaptable voice'. At the end of the article there was one brief mention of her daughter: 'Sylvia, who lived in the Mutley area of Plymouth, leaves a 15-year-old daughter.'

Just around the time of her mother's death, Vanessa was living with a neighbour in Crozier Road. Eventually Vanessa moved in with her Aunt Valerie in Salisbury Avenue, St Jude, on the far side of the city. But Valerie found Vanessa hard to handle. The teenager had huge mood swings and was quite clearly bottling up a lot of rage about the death of her mother.

If Roger Marks had hoped his ex-wife's death might bring about a reconciliation with his estranged daughter, he was to be disappointed. Following Sylvia's death, a family court decided he was not suitable to raise his teenaged daughter. Instead, her grandparents Kath and Bert Budge were given custody.

Roger Marks's take on what happened with his ex-wife's family is tainted with bitterness. 'After Sylvia died her family started worrying that I might get custody of Vanessa, which would have meant I'd get back the house in Crozier Road which I'd given to Sylvia when we split up. That's why they fought for custody of Vanessa. I lost because I couldn't provide assurances I would be around to look after her while I was trying to keep down a day job.'

He continued: 'They used Vanessa as a pawn in a sense

because they were determined to hold onto that house and then sell it and keep all the cash from it, which is precisely what they did.'

Losing a parent is hard at any age, but for Vanessa, an overweight, lonely child, losing her adored mother at the crucial age of fifteen would perhaps turn out to be a blow from which she never really recovered.

Family members and close friends believe that Vanessa 'changed virtually overnight' after her mother died. One old friend explained: 'Vanessa and her mother were incredibly close up until her death. It was almost as if it was a case of Sylvia and Vanessa against the world. They'd survived since Roger left them and in some ways thrived. OK, there may have been those problems with baby-sitters but Sylvia and Vanessa only really had each other so they got through all the good and bad times as one unit. The trouble was that after Sylvia died Vanessa became much more sullen and withdrawn. It was almost as if she felt she had been abandoned by her mother. Neither of them had been particularly close to Granny Kath or the rest of her mother's family because Sylvia was considered a bit of a law unto herself, always going off singing with that pop group, and some other members of the family, including her own sisters, disapproved of her lifestyle and the way she left Vanessa on her own at home for long periods of time.'

And Vanessa's Uncle Barry said Vanessa 'became a much more snappy, ill-tempered person after her mother's death but that's hardly surprising. She must have been in a state of delayed shock for years after Sylvia died.'

After Sylvia's death her former husband drifted away from Plymouth and he admits not seeing much of Vanessa. It must have been a severe double blow to an already fragile child, who had been bottling up her feelings.

To make matters worse, Sylvia's mother, Kath Budge, sensed that Vanessa would be 'quite a handful'. 'Vanessa wasn't one of those kids you took to immediately and so the family were dreading looking after her in many ways after Sylvia died,' said one relative.

Vanessa was now a sullen, overweight, tomboyish-looking teenager. She'd already spent some time at her Aunt Valerie's house in St Jude and now she was expected to live with her elderly grandmother and grandfather in their small terraced house at 12 Wellington Street, near the centre of Plymouth, where they'd moved from Grey-stokes Road a few years earlier.

A relative later described how 'Vanessa was in many ways a typical teenager but she was also extremely fragile after the loss of her mother. Soon she was clashing with Kath and there were long sulks. Everyone soon found it very difficult to cope with Vanessa's stubbornness.'

One neighbour in Wellington Street recalled finding Vanessa sitting staring into space on the doorstep of the little house one day. 'Earlier I'd heard a lot of shouting and screaming from inside the house and there was Vanessa, who was a large girl, sitting on the doorstep like a lost little child. I asked her if she was all right and she didn't even answer me. I felt really sorry for her.'

Other relatives said that Kath and her surviving daughters were shocked at Vanessa's bad manners. They put a lot of it down to Sylvia's lack of parental guidance before she died. 'Vanessa lacked all the basic ingredients to make her a well brought-up child. These days you would call her almost feral, I suppose. Vanessa could hardly hold a knife and fork properly and she wore the same clothes for days on end and seemed to lack the most basic personal hygiene. Sylvia might have been a happy, easy-going person on the outside, but she had been a highly irresponsible parent in many ways. She hadn't guided Vanessa in terms of the most basic parental skills. It was almost as if she had just left Vanessa to her own devices a lot of the time.'

Inevitably, when the concerned family tried to instil some basic manners into the still deeply bereaved teenager, it sparked a tirade of abuse and anger which effectively made Vanessa even harder to control. 'Vanessa just wasn't like most other kids. She was physically large and she looked more like a boy than a girl to start with. That meant other children were quite cruel to her and she suffered a lot of taunting in the playground.'

Another relative who attended some of the family get-togethers at the time said recently: 'Vanessa was better at being with adults than children in many ways. She seemed more relaxed in their company.' But behind her hesitant smile, the large, awkward teenager had learned how to manipulate many of her mother's friends.

One of them later explained: 'Vanessa was disarmingly open and almost flirtatious from her early teens. It was quite disturbing to watch her in action. She would think nothing of giving a male member of the family a cuddle, and remember we are talking about a large girl of fifteen here, not a toddler. None of the family said anything at the time because we were all too worried about causing her any additional upset following the death of her mother, but looking back on it, there were some very clear danger signs as to her attitude towards men.'

One neighbour in Wellington Street who attended a party at Kath's house shortly after Sylvia's death recalled: 'Vanessa was just too over-friendly for a teenager. She'd plonk herself on people's laps as if she was a little girl. But she was heavy and very grown-up for her age and some of the men felt very awkward about her behaviour.'

And throughout this period in her life, Vanessa never once mentioned the abuse she received at the hands of at least one of her late mother's 'baby-sitters'. Vanessa must have realized that in order to survive it was important to keep moving. Never look back. She had long since learned not to trust anyone. Even back then as a lonely teenager, Vanessa knew full well that if she wanted something she would have to go out and get it all on her own. But that was fine by her. It meant that she could thrive in her own little world, away from the stark realities and rules of the outside world. Bottling up what had happened with those 'baby-sitters' was part of her character. She only revealed what she wanted to reveal.

Grandmother Kath found it so hard bringing up Vanessa that she was, to a certain extent, neglected and left to fend for herself in Wellington Street. Vanessa had put on even more weight and was a typical teenager with an awkward manner. Some complained that she mumbled so much that it was difficult to understand what she was actually saying.

Undoubtedly, some of those childhood experiences had made a very distinct mark on Vanessa's mind, as well as on her body. She just didn't trust people and why should she?

In Vanessa's own special 'life bubble' she could do whatever she wanted and there wasn't a thing anyone else could do about it. True, she played on the pity that she received from her family after her mother's death but what none of her relatives realized was that her sullen, dark moods were connected to her dogged determination to be a law unto herself.

But as the husband of one of Vanessa's closest surviving relatives said recently: 'It doesn't matter what happened to Vanessa as a child, it still doesn't give her the right to destroy people's lives in the way she has done. Everyone tried to help Vanessa after her mother died and she rejected us all.'

So Vanessa Marks, now aged fifteen – and in the words of some 'virtually a feral child' – found herself playing outside her grandmother's house in Wellington Street after moving there following that short spell at Aunt Valerie's house. No wonder she started to get into trouble. And of course Kath Budge had a lot more on her mind besides her wayward granddaughter. She'd been shattered by the death from cancer of two of her four beloved daughters. As one of her oldest friends later recalled: 'It weighed on Kath's mind so much after they died. No parent wants to outlive their children and Kath had already been to the funeral of two of her daughters.'

Then to add to her anxieties, Kath's husband Bert was becoming increasingly ill, leaving Granny Kath Budge feeling even more isolated and lonely – not the sort of person who should have been given the responsibility of looking after a complicated teenaged girl who'd just lost her own mother at such an early age.

Kath threw herself into her housework and always kept the house immaculate, which made Vanessa feel even more like a stranger in what was supposed to be her home. The two inevitably clashed over Vanessa's inability to clear up and help with the housework. Soon she and her grandmother were barely on speaking terms.

'Vanessa would just disappear for hours on end when she wasn't at school and I don't think Kath was all that bothered. She was just relieved to get Vanessa out of the house so she could give it a clean-up,' remembered one neighbour in Wellington Street.

Sometimes Kath would go and have a drink in the Fawn pub near the house in Wellington Street. One regular at the pub later recalled: 'Kath was a right funny character. She'd come in here, order a half of stout and then sit and watch all the regulars come in and out before polishing off her drink and leaving. She just seemed happy to be amongst people and to get away from her granddaughter. She said the girl was driving her mad. Mind you, Kath always had something to say about everyone and sometimes she was a bit blunt but she usually had a smile on her face come rain or shine.'

The strained atmosphere inside that small house in Wellington Street went from bad to worse when Vanessa started to become closer to her father Roger's two sisters – her aunts – Linda and Janet. They had stepped in where their brother had failed. Both Linda and Janet were very concerned about Vanessa and how she was coping with the loss of her mother. As one of Kath's oldest friends later recalled: 'Linda and Janet were just trying to help. They knew that Vanessa was something of a handful and they wanted to take the strain off Kath to a certain degree.'

But Kath Budge was irritated that her daughter's ex-husband's family should even try to get close to Vanessa. She detested Roger Marks for what he had done to her daughter many years earlier. So when aunts Linda and Janet offered to take Vanessa off to a Butlins holiday camp in Somerset, Kath Budge was furious. At first she tried to refuse to allow Vanessa to go but Vanessa would have none of it. She was determined to go on holiday and had grown very fond of both her aunts on her father's side. Other family and friends noticed that Vanessa's surly behaviour actually improved after she started 'bonding' with members of her father's family. Yet Roger Marks was – by his own admission – rarely involved with his daughter at this time.

Vanessa's Uncle Barry was well aware, like many other members of the family, that Vanessa and her grandmother were at loggerheads at this time. 'It was clear from our visits to the house in Wellington Street. It was sad because Vanessa was only a child then and maybe she needed some care and patience but she and Kath just did not hit it off.'

Inevitably, Vanessa's problems at home with Granny Kath went from bad to worse, as she turned to food for comfort to make up for the dreadful atmosphere at home in Wellington Street. One of Kath's neighbours in Wellington Street later said: 'Vanessa had seemed so happy as a child before her mother's death but she started to put on even more weight after Sylvia died. She always seemed to be playing on her own. You could see there was an inner sadness about Vanessa. I felt very sorry for her.'

But, most disturbingly, Vanessa was spending an increasing amount of time away from the house and Kath Budge didn't always know where she was.

Many friends and family members have since wondered whether, if Vanessa had had professional help back then, she might not have developed into such a dark character, so prepared later to cause pain and anguish to others without seeming to care.

Vanessa was having so much difficulty coping with the reality of never seeing her mother Sylvia again that she started researching into the paranormal. It was to become a long-term fascination. She was obsessed with the idea of communicating with her mother beyond the grave. She had so many questions she wanted to ask her. Why had she left her at such a young age? The young Vanessa convinced herself that Sylvia would one day try to get in touch with her to 'explain' why she left her. It sounded more like a desperate plea for help from a lost and helpless teenage girl.

One of the few real friends Vanessa had during those difficult years after her mother's death was a local teenage boy called Andrew George. He was a soft, sensitive character who seemed genuinely prepared to listen to what Vanessa had to say. Vanessa had never met a boy who was actually able to make proper conversation, and unlike other boys he wasn't just 'after one thing', either. In some ways Andrew – or 'Drew' as she liked to call him – became like the brother she never had because he was always looking out for her and making sure she got home safely.

Over the next couple of years, Vanessa and Drew became very close pals and in many ways that friendship enabled Vanessa to outwardly start coming to terms with her mother's premature death. Vanessa became once more – on the outside at least – that same ebullient, larger-than-life character she'd appeared to be before the death of her mother, although her father would later claim she never really found happiness following Sylvia's death. But if that really is the case, Vanessa hid it very well.

Academically, though, Vanessa did not exactly shine. She quit school at sixteen and went to work in a number of different jobs, ending up as a secretary in a local building company. But she found life much happier after leaving school. It's not clear how much longer she lived with her grandmother Kath in Wellington Street but by all accounts Vanessa spent as little time as possible in the small, cramped house. She and Drew would hang out in the local pubs and clubs and she would even go back to Drew's parents' home nearby. They were always kind and welcoming towards her.

At eighteen, Vanessa officially inherited £10,000, which was the proceeds from the sale of that house in Crozier Road that the Budge family had held on to after Sylvia's death. It was far from a fortune, but to a young girl who'd never had much it was like winning the lottery. Some eighteen-year-olds might have frittered the money away on clothes and cars or holidays abroad, but perhaps in an attempt to provide herself with the security she'd lacked as a child, Vanessa invested her windfall in bricks and mortar, buying a modest home in Douglass Road, Efford, where she hoped to live happily ever after.

In 1988 one of Kath Budge's old neighbours from Greystokes Road bumped into Kath in Plymouth city centre during a protest against Margaret Thatcher's notorious poll tax. The neighbour recalled: 'I hadn't seen her for years so we stopped and had a long chat. I asked her how her granddaughter was and she said they weren't living together any more. They had fallen out. Kath's exact words were: "My granddaughter's gone. I didn't get on with her. She was nasty." '

Then Kath Budge added: 'She's a horrible piece of work.'

The neighbour continued: 'I never forgot that remark because it seemed such a harsh thing to say about your own granddaughter.'

So it was hardly surprising that Vanessa had left Wellington Street and Granny Kath behind once and for all. Later Vanessa – perhaps surprisingly – told one close friend that despite the arguments with Kath, she was very grateful to her grandmother for looking after her following her mother's death. But she knew that they were destined never to get on well. 'We're like peas out of the same pod,' Vanessa told her friend.

Meanwhile, her friendship with Andrew George was developing slowly but surely into something much more serious. Drew was a couple of years older than her but he and Vanessa shared so many interests and were capable of talking to each other until the cows came home. She was determined not to lose Andrew George so she was delighted when their friendship finally turned into a fully blown romance.

The district of Efford, where Vanessa had bought her house, was regarded locally as one of the better places in Plymouth for young families to live. It was a mostly residential area with a population of around 5,000, and its inhabitants tended to be families who'd lived in Plymouth for generations and were proud of its community feel and low crime levels. As with many close-knit communities, outsiders were regarded with suspicion and there was universal outcry when the City Council earmarked local land as a possible site for a permanent gypsy and traveller site.

Vanessa soon settled into the area and turned her recently acquired house in Douglass Road into a comfortable home. It had three bedrooms and even a car port big enough for one vehicle in front of the house. In Vanessa's terms it was a 'desirable property'. She'd been working as a secretary at that local building company for quite some time and was thinking seriously about having a family of her own. She was hoping that one day she'd settle down with Drew and live a happy, normal life a long way from her turbulent, transient childhood.

Vanessa told her relatives at the time that she was determined not to move house ever again. She'd done too much of that sort of thing during her childhood. Now she wanted some stability in her life.

Soon she was virtually living with Andrew George at the

house in Douglass Road. To Vanessa it must have seemed like a dream come true. A good person, Drew had become the most important figure in her life. She'd got herself a reasonably well-paid job. Life as an adult was already turning out to be a lot more enjoyable than being a child.

PART TWO
A Happy Life

'Happiness is an imaginary condition, formerly often attributed by the living to the dead, now usually attributed by adults to children, and by children to adults.'

Thomas Szasz

4

Vanessa and her teenage sweetheart Andrew George married on 23 April 1993, when Vanessa was twenty-three years old. The register was signed by Andrew's grandmother, Dorothy. Vanessa's own family were not much in evidence at the wedding or the small party held back at their house in Douglass Road afterwards. By this stage of George's life only two of the Budge sisters – Valerie and Janet – were still alive and there appears to have been little contact, if any, between any of them.

The new 'Vanessa George' was ecstatically happy to have got married for many reasons but first and foremost she believed that Andrew George – 'Drew'– was her soulmate as well as her lover and she had at last found true happiness after years of hiding her misery from everyone in the outside world. They also happened to have a very lively sex life, according to Drew.

George had already made it clear she fully intended to start a family almost immediately so it was no surprise to family and friends when she announced she was pregnant at virtually the same time as the wedding. She saw marriage and children as prerequisites for getting away from her past, to put as much distance between herself and her childhood as she could manage. Many people brought up in difficult conditions seem to do likewise, so it's no great surprise.

Those who knew her back in the early days of her marriage say that George seemed almost obsessed with having kids. 'She was utterly determined to have children as quickly as possible,' said one former friend. Within weeks of getting pregnant, George was proudly showing off her slight bump to anyone who seemed interested. To her, it was an achievement, probably the most important achievement of her life to date.

During those early days of marriage, according to Andrew George, the couple enjoyed a close relationship, with George finally discovering the intimacy she'd been searching for since her mum died. She was pregnant for much of that period but this apparently did little to quell the couple's sexual appetite.

'We had a very loving relationship – and a pretty good sex life too,' Andrew George later remarked. 'She was my soulmate – we were besotted. Every morning before I'd go to work we'd have a cuddle and a kiss. We'd say, "I love you", and, "Have a groovy day." She'd send me texts or give me a call to see how the day was going. Saying, "How you doing, love? See you later."

'Most days when I came home we'd have a hug and a kiss. I'd walk in through the door, and she'd come to hug me, and I'd be like "Hang on, let me get my boots off first." I'd call her my Poppy after the flower. She liked that.'

By all accounts, George grew enormous during pregnancy but, in fairness to Drew, he was never once critical of her weight gain. As one family friend later described: 'Drew just wasn't the type of character to make a fuss. He was just very happy for Vanessa because he knew how much she'd wanted to start a family as soon as they married.'

Their daughters Pearl and Grace were born in quick succession, 'home delivery style', at the family house in Douglass Road and it appears the births were not complicated. It must have seemed to George that she was a natural mother, despite all those childhood ghosts. Maybe she really had found her true vocation in life?

She was almost nonchalant when talking about the obvious physical agonies of childbirth. One old friend later said: 'Vanessa just shrugged her shoulders and got on with having babies. She said it was no big deal but she was obviously immensely proud of her babies and being a mum.'

At every opportunity George showed off her baby daughters to neighbours, friends and family. George adored the attention that being a mother gave her and she felt that settling down to life as a loving mother and wife was the best thing she could ever have done. It really suited her and she dreaded the idea of going back to work as a secretary, although she knew she needed to contribute towards the household in order for her and Andrew to survive financially.

George became a familiar figure out and about with her daughters when they were toddlers and, in the words of one neighbour in Douglass Road: 'She had a confident way about her. A relaxed, happy-go-lucky manner, which made us all like her around here. Vanessa didn't seem fazed by anything.'

Other relatives and friends regularly bumped into George at the local bingo hall. 'Vanessa was friendly and bubbly but she always had a serious look on her face once the chatting stopped and the bingo calling began,' commented one former neighbour, who met George there.

But what no one realized was that George's soul had long been crushed by many of the traumatic events of her childhood. She'd long since become an expert at putting on her 'happy face' to all her family and friends but beneath that glossy exterior lay a distant heart.

George knew only too well that she could get everything she wanted if she put on this charming exterior. People would trust her and like her if she was jolly and happy. And to a certain degree she was happy. Well a lot happier than she had been during her childhood. She loved and adored her husband Drew, especially the way he didn't question her past. He was a genuinely nice guy who never looked beneath the surface of anything. 'He's a handsome-looking devil, too,' she'd say to some of her friends and family at that time.

Andrew George saw in Vanessa a good-natured, caring mother to their children and the person he truly and genuinely loved. She seemed like a woman who, as they say, 'just got on with it'. He thought he could see how good a person she was by the way she looked after Pearl and Grace.

George herself continued to relish the status of being a mother. It gave her access to people and she adored the way other mothers looked up to her because she seemed to have such a relaxed manner. In short, she gave the outward impression of being incredibly capable. She was carefully moulding herself into the exact opposite of her own mother. She would never go off singing in a pub band like her mother did. She would never leave her children alone in the hands of a baby-sitter.

George adored the camaraderie with other new mums, to whom she'd often natter for hours on the phone or in the street near the family home. A lot of people told her she was a natural-born carer. It made George start to think seriously about retraining to work in childcare. She convinced herself she had a natural affinity towards children. Maybe a lot of that was down to her own lost childhood. She thought she related better to children, even though there had been very few of them around when she was a girl. It was certainly true that the ghosts of her early years were making her resent adults for all the things they had put her through.

George also found her job as a secretary deeply unfulfilling. It seemed a natural step from the birth of her daughters to the childcare business. All her friends and neighbours reckoned she'd be perfect. The pay wasn't going to be as good as that of a secretary, but that didn't matter to her. She liked the idea of a job that revolved around children and where parents would be in debt to her for looking after their kids. George longed to be popular after a childhood peppered with loneliness and playground bullying.

George was delighted when her application to work as an assistant at the Efford pre-school, near her home, was accepted. It had just benefited from a £3,500 National Lottery grant to buy new equipment for the children, and the staff convinced her she was joining them at a very exciting time in its development.

In 1996 George's Aunt Janet died from cancer at the age of just forty-nine. It was another dreadful blow for the now elderly Kath Budge, who had lost three of her four daughters to cancer. The funeral of Janet – wife to George's uncle, Barry Medway – was overshadowed by the fact that many close family members and friends were now convinced that the cancer gene was going to doom every single female in her family to an early death. The only surviving sister, Valerie, remained healthy, although serious illness would eventually catch up with her as well.

One old neighbour and friend of the Budge family who attended Janet's funeral in 1996 recalled: 'Once again we saw Kath at one of her daughters' funerals. Janet's funeral wasn't too morbid because she had been very open about her illness and didn't want it to be a sad occasion. We had tea and sandwiches at the house she shared with her husband Barry, but Kath was almost too distraught to speak.'

Friends and relatives saw no sign of George at her aunt's funeral. One family member remembered: 'Someone actually pointed it out at the time and defended Vanessa by saying that she would have found it hard to be at Janet's funeral because it would have reminded her of her mother Sylvia's death.'

Janet's husband Barry didn't see much of his wife's family after her death in 1996, although he admitted recently: 'Apart from family parties I didn't exactly see much of them in the old days, either, but at one stage I did see more of Vanessa than the others because she used to play with my son Lee when he was young as they were virtually the same age.' George's cousin, Lee Medway, had even been a regular visitor to Sylvia and Vanessa's home in Crozier Road. That was when Barry had first heard about those 'problems' with the baby-sitters.

But despite the image George presented of an outgoing mum devoted to her young family, things in Douglass Road were not all they seemed and cracks were already beginning to show on the surface of her marriage to Andrew. After their starting off as 'soulmates', Andrew and Vanessa George's relationship had become steadily more volatile. Andrew George later claimed that in 1996 – three years after they married – George started sleeping with one of his closest friends.

'She had an affair in 1996 which I only found out about six years later,' he says now. 'I guess that shows how devious she can be, and how good she is at keeping secrets. I found out through a friend of hers and it really hurt.'

Predictably, Andrew George's knee-jerk reaction was to return tit for tat. 'I went on a revenge thing, I suppose, to make myself feel better. I ended up sleeping with other women. We called a truce and said we'd start again. But it took at least five years before it stopped hurting.'

People often say that a relationship never truly returns to how it was following infidelity, but the Georges did their best to put it behind them, continuing to enjoy an active love life despite Vanessa George's ballooning figure. Never exactly slim, she had piled on the pounds throughout her adult life until she topped the scales at nearly eighteen stone. She'd also become virtually addicted to sunbeds and her skin had taken on a strange, orange pallor most of the time.

But the couple's sex life continued to blossom despite all the 'setbacks'. Her husband remembers: 'If we fancied it we'd go for it. Yes, I think the attraction was fading. She put on a bit of weight, and she was spending too much time on sunbeds, and starting to look bad from that. But I'm not a shallow guy. You can see people for what they are inside. We had some nice times. We'd still tell each other, "I love you."'

A photograph of George appeared in the 'community news' section of the *Plymouth Herald* in November 1998. It showed her surrounded by young children, with three sitting on her lap. The article noted she was 'completing an NVQ in childcare' and had written a poem to promote the pre-school group, which was struggling with dwindling numbers. Her poem was to be used to 'highlight facilities and hopefully attract new children'.

Having completed that NVQ level 2 in childcare, George started working as a teaching assistant at the nearby Laira Green primary school. That job came to an end, but she was recommended so highly by the school that she was offered a position at the adjoining nursery, called Little Ted's. Children in the nursery were aged between two and five, but youngsters up to eleven could attend breakfast and after-school clubs.

Little Ted's day nursery ran two units – unit 1 next to

Laira Green primary school and unit 2 at Laira United Church, both in Bramley Road. It was managed by Angela Chudley. Operating for many years, it was a well-known institution in the area and there were few families in the neighbourhood who did not have some connection to it.

An Ofsted report for unit 1, in 2007, revealed that the quality and standards of the care and nursery education at Little Ted's were 'satisfactory'. Inspectors said that the provision for 'protecting children from harm or neglect and helping them stay safe' was also 'satisfactory'. The report added: 'Use of risk assessments and vigilant supervision by staff reduces potential hazards for children within the setting.'

An Ofsted report for unit 2, published in 2008, said that the provision for 'protecting children from harm or neglect and helping them stay safe' at the nursery was 'good' and that 'Children are safe and secure within the nursery premises.' The overall rating for unit 2 was 'good'.

With the nursery and school sharing premises, there were plenty of crossovers between the two and parents of early-years primary children were delighted their kids still got to see the familiar, reassuring face of their bubbly, outgoing former teaching assistant Vanessa George to give them that extra continuity and security.

At Little Ted's, George's open, friendly demeanour soon made her a favourite among staff and parents alike. So trusted and so capable, she was soon rated as the nursery's deputy Special Educational Needs Coordinator.

Back home, however, George was finding herself far

less popular. Her long-suffering grandmother, Kath Budge, made a point of telling all their relatives and friends how much she preferred her husband Andrew to her. Kath adored Andrew and would proudly tell anyone who'd listen what a hard-working fellow he was and how he was on call twenty-four hours a day for his job as a heating engineer and he worked long hours. One family friend said how 'Kath was very impressed with Andrew and in some ways she seemed almost surprised that Vanessa had got herself such a good "catch".'

Other friends and relatives felt similarly about George's husband. One recalled: 'We all wondered what on earth he saw in Vanessa. She was already about twice his size by this time and while they were undoubtedly a loving couple, they didn't exactly match each other physically. He was slim and tall and rather handsome and almost dapper, while Vanessa looked like an orange whale after the birth of her daughters and too much time under a sunbed. Much of the time she also looked as if she hadn't bothered to get properly dressed of a morning.'

Sadly George's relationship with her grandmother was deteriorating fast. When Kath suffered an agonizing bout of cancer of the lip, from which she eventually made a full recovery following a number of painful operations, it did little to improve the relationship. 'It was sad to see how badly they got on,' said one of Kath's oldest friends. 'Even when Kath was going through all her lip cancer problems, neither of them seemed capable of improving things between themselves.' George would sometimes pop round to Wellington Street with her two little daughters but she hardly ever exchanged a proper word of conversation with her grandmother.

Kath Budge adored George's two daughters, Pearl and Grace. 'If it had not been for them then I'm not sure Kath and Vanessa would have seen each other at all,' added Kath's friend. 'I think Kath saw Pearl and Grace as replacements for her own daughters in a way. There was nothing twisted about it. She got a lot of pleasure out of spoiling those girls and who can blame her?'

When George visited Kath's house in Wellington Street with her two children she'd often only drop them off and then return later to collect them. It seems likely that part of the problem was the childhood memories associated with that house where George was forced to live following her mother's death. But, as one of Kath's oldest friends later explained, there may have been other, more twisted reasons behind George's cold attitude towards her grandmother's relationship with her daughters.

'I think Vanessa was in many ways jealous of her daughters' relationship with Kath, who seemed to be much nicer to them than she had ever been back in those difficult times after Sylvia's death,' said Kath's friend.

Kath showered her two great-grandchildren with gifts whenever they visited, which left George fuming quietly to herself. According to Kath's old friend: 'You could see the way Vanessa's head was working. She'd turn up to get the girls and find Kath poring over Pearl and Grace, giving them money and sweets all the time. Vanessa's face would look like thunder.' Other times when George remained at the house in Wellington Street she'd just get up in the middle of a visit and make the girls leave the house early for no real reason. 'Kath would be heartbroken but no one ever said anything,' said Kath's friend. 'We all suspected what was behind it all. Kath and Vanessa had never got on, never seen eye to eye, but then a lot of that was down to them being so similar. Kath could be very rude and very blunt but she had a good heart. I'm not sure the same could ever be said for Vanessa, though.'

Occasionally, George would reluctantly take her grandmother out in her car on shopping trips. But as a measure of their mutual dislike, George would make the old lady pay for the petrol in her car. 'Vanessa would also make Kath pay for all the shopping when they went out. It was outrageous. No wonder Kath disliked her so much,' a family friend recalled.

Meanwhile Granny Kath continued to spoil and pamper Pearl and Grace. A couple of years after her daughter Janet's death, Kath announced she was giving her great-granddaughters £10,000 to be put in a trust for when they turned eighteen. After her own brush with cancer, Kath had cannily decided to make sure that she gave away her money in such a way that the taxman might not get his hands on it when she died. She had a healthy nest-egg built up from her previous savings combined with the money from the sale of a house in Tavistock which her husband Bert had inherited.

'Kath wanted to hand out the money early to avoid death duties. Kath had worked down at the iron factory during her marriage to Bert and even saved up her own money, as well as from the sale of that house. She kept it all hidden away but decided it was better to bring it out to share with her family before she died,' said one of Kath's oldest friends later.

George was furious when she first heard about her grandmother's plans but then got the surprise of her life when Kath decided the money could go to her if it was spent on something 'for the family'. Kath's old friend recalled: 'That was typical of Kath. She decided it was only fair that the money should go towards something that would benefit the whole family.'

George agreed to use the £10,000 on buying a caravan at the Harlyn Sands Holiday Park, near Padstow, in Cornwall. It was a couple of hours' drive north-west from Plymouth and would be the perfect weekend and holiday retreat for her and her young family.

Kath Budge was delighted if somewhat relieved that her granddaughter really had decided to buy something with the cash which all her family could enjoy. 'That made Kath feel better about Vanessa because at least she was buying something the whole family could use,' added Kath's old friend.

What no one could ever have envisaged was how George would later use that same caravan site to feed her own sick and twisted desires.

5

In a bid to earn some extra income, Vanessa George the nursery assistant began offering her baby-sitting services not just to the parents at Little Ted's but also to her fellow staff, some of whom even had their own children at the same nursery where she worked. One childminder who knew George recalled: 'She was a lovely woman, very talkative and bubbly and very pleasant. Everyone liked her. It seemed only natural that she would do baby-sitting. A lot of staff at nursery schools do it to make some extra cash.'

By this time many of the mothers knew the 'rather large' classroom assistant at Little Ted's as 'Vee'. She had already seen a generation of local children through nursery school and socialized in the evenings with some of their parents. She was often to be found horsing around to raise a smile from kids and colleagues. Photos taken at the time show her wearing newspaper stuck to her face and a pair of false lips made from the red rind of a cheese snack during one children's party. A former colleague at Little Ted's said: 'That was typical Vanessa. She was never afraid to play the clown.'

One mother who regarded George as a friend said: 'She seemed lovely, really friendly and always happy to help. She seemed like an angel – someone warm and really easy to get on with.'

So well-regarded was George that every Thursday – when Little Ted's was shut – she provided childcare for working parents at her home in Douglass Road, despite not being officially registered as a childminder. She received £4.50 an hour to look after up to five children aged between twelve months and three years.

A former friend, Patricia Gilbery, a childminder, also cared for four of the children before and after school hours and would drop them off at and collect them from George's house on those days. Now, with the benefit of hindsight, she shudders at what might have been going on at her friend Vee's house during those six long hours: 'There were times I picked up those children from Vee's house and one of the babies might have been crying. At the time you put it down to one of them just being ratty, hungry or tired and think nothing of it.'

Nobody who worked at Little Ted's had any reason to believe George was anything other than what she appeared – a fun-loving, boisterous good-time girl. Even her interest in the paranormal, which hadn't waned since she'd first looked into it after her mum's death, didn't cause concern. Plenty of people believe in ghosts and the afterlife and to George's family and friends it was nothing more than a harmless hobby.

But inside George's head a lot of conflicting messages were driving her to distraction. She was about to pass the age her mother was when she died. It was a milestone in many ways. George had very mixed emotions about her mother. She loved and adored her for looking after her but she couldn't shake off that feeling of abandonment, which had been with her since the day her mother got sick. One close relative explained: 'Vanessa was fighting all sorts of demons and when she got to the same age as her mother had been when she died she found it even harder to cope but you'd never realize from her outward appearance. She just laughed and joked around but it was all an act.'

Over the years, George had become virtually addicted to the various satellite TV programmes about ghosts and the paranormal which dominated the television listings at certain times of the day and night. This almost obsessive interest combined with passing the milestone age that her mother was when she died had led George to become much more serious about hunting for ghosts and she was determined to 'make contact' with her dead mother. Her fascination with the paranormal was so genuine in her mind that she often boasted to her friends at Little Ted's that she could see and speak to the dead. They mostly ignored the bubbly, overweight George and put it all down to her eccentricity.

So George began attending séances and trying to get in touch with the spirit world. She soon claimed to have contacted the ghost of a man who'd died 200 years ago. By 2005 she was going to all-night ghost hunts at least once a month and was even captured on film for a TV documentary with members of a group she'd joined called 'Haunted Devon'. The programme was never actually broadcast.

A Plymouth-based television producer, David James, worked with the Haunted Devon group on a number of psychic 'events' through his company, Encore Productions, in 2005 and 2006. He met George on numerous occasions: 'Vanessa seemed very bright and jolly. She was like everyone else in that she could make you laugh but she also could be quite stern. We called her "Mrs George" most of the time.'

At one stage in late 2005 David James went with George and other members of Haunted Devon to the notorious Shaugh Tunnel, a disused Victorian railway tunnel in the centre of Devon which was renowned for psychic 'events'. George and her fellow 'researchers' spent hours in the damp, pitch-black tunnel setting up Ouija boards and trying to get in touch with the spirits of the dead, including George's mother Sylvia.

David James said that after working with George and other enthusiasts his whole attitude towards psychic phenomena changed. 'The trouble with Vanessa and many of the other people is that they are looking for something they want to find so they usually find it. But that doesn't really mean there is anything truly psychic out there.'

George and her fellow 'seekers' were later also filmed posing on the ornate staircase at a haunted manor house called Buckland Filleigh, in Beaworthy, Devon, in 2006. One friend from her ghost-hunting days later said: 'Vanessa often told us she could see ghosts. She said she was open to new things. She would stay up all night looking for ghosts, then when the investigation was over she'd go to the pub with everyone. She was pretty popular with the other members, just a really nice girl.'

George was on the books of Haunted Devon from 2006 until around September 2008, but she rarely attended from around mid-2007. Other members later described George as 'fun' but added that she was 'perhaps a little bit bawdy'. One member said: 'She gave no indication what she was like. She was a character who wanted to be the centre of attention. But she would also talk to you as if you were her mates.'

Haunted Devon insist they are a serious group of people with a strong interest in investigating 'the paranormal'. According to one member: 'We're primarily a research organization, dedicated to trying to find the true cause of paranormal activity. It's not about seeing ghosts or dead people – we're looking into the science of it.'

The member added: 'George was typical of so many people out there. She'd watched *Most Haunted* on one of the satellite channels and decided that this was what she wanted to do. She joined with a friend who had an interest in the spiritual field, attending tarot readings, that sort of stuff. They got into it because they thought it was an exciting venture – being involved in investigations. She [VG] appeared to be a very normal housewife who simply came, like so many others, to try to learn more about what's going on.'

George also visited the grave of Kitty Jay, a servant girl in the late eighteenth century, who was apparently raped by the son of the household where she worked and became pregnant. George made a point of emphasizing to Haunted Devon members how close she was to her own family. One member said: 'She came along quite a few times in the first few months but then it tailed off. A lot of it was down to getting baby-sitters. She was quite a family-orientated person and if you asked her to go on an investigation she would say, "Oh, I have to leave early." It showed that she cared about her own kids. We saw her very public face, her going-out face, her social face.'

In the middle of 2007 George's long-held obsession with getting in touch with her dead mother reached new heights. She had long been determined to 'find' her mother and try to establish why she 'left' her at such an early age, but she had always been very careful not to admit openly what she was doing.

George also took part in a séance at a 600-year-old pub called the Minerva Inn in the centre of Plymouth. It was a bizarre evening, even by her standards. She and ten other paranormal 'researchers' descended on the rickety old inn and headed for a corner of the bar, where they sat in silence as a psychic tried to make contact with various dead people, including George's mother Sylvia.

George had persuaded the Haunted Devon team to visit the Minerva Inn because it was one of her mother's favourite venues when she was a singer. One regular at the pub later recalled: 'Oh, we all remember Vanessa George well. She was huge and very lumbersome but she had a really wicked sense of humour, even though they were all looking very serious about their séance. We get loads of psychic types in here but she stuck out because she seemed much less tense than most of them usually are.'

These days the Haunted Devon group has long since dissociated itself from George and her activities.

Having spent much of 2005, 2006 and 2007 trying to make 'contact' with her dead mother, George became disillusioned with the paranormal and in 2007 chose instead to make email 'contact' with some much more disturbing *living* people. These would eventually turn out to be more evil forces than anything she would find in a séance. They would lead her into a life of unimaginable depravity.

George was brilliant at throwing people with her bubbly, seemingly relaxed attitude towards life. Many at this time were entranced by her apparent spirit and energy. And she gave exactly that impression at Harlyn Sands Holiday Park, near Padstow, Cornwall, where the family owned the caravan bought with the £10,000 provided by Granny Kath. When George wasn't busy on either her laptop or her mobile phone, both of which seemed to take up a huge amount of her time, the friendly, caring nursery worker often volunteered as a 'parent helper' at the park's children's club to the delight of full-time staff.

'To all the staff, she was just a mum who liked helping out,' remembered Leon McHugh, the campsite's former entertainments manager. Nothing was too much trouble for the larger-than-life Plymouth mum. She'd willingly help change nappies, undress the children for swimming and play dressing-up games. 'She came across as a person who just loved children,' recalled McHugh.

Only one incident made Leon McHugh wonder whether there was a darker side to the ever-smiling Mrs George. 'We were playing on the park's pirate ship,' he said. 'One boy hit another, the sort of falling out you get with kids. Vanessa smacked his bottom really hard and he started crying. I told her she shouldn't have done it, but she just told me he'd deserved it.'

However, George soon switched back into the caring, cheerful mother of two everyone had come to know and the incident was quickly forgotten. The George family would often be seen making the most of the entertainment on offer at the caravan park and Vanessa and Andrew weren't above putting on full fancy dress and dancing around to a Coldplay tribute band at the Halloween disco.

There is no doubt that granny Kath Budge nursed a broken heart about her three dead daughters right up until the day in December 2007 when cancer finally took her life as well. Earlier, she'd fought off lip cancer only to then be taken by stomach cancer. It really did seem as if a cancer gene was running rampant through the female members of her family.

But sadly Kath's latest battle with cancer did little to help improve the relationship between George and her grandmother. A few weeks before Kath died from the cancer that had ravaged her body, grandmother and granddaughter had a bad row about money. George told her grandmother she would not go to her funeral. Kath tried to put a brave face on it and even told one of her closest friends shortly before she died: 'I know Vanessa hates me. She is a greedy, evil person and I never want anything to do with her ever again. I don't even care if she comes to my funeral or not.'

But Kath's old friend later recalled: 'Of course, Kath was trying to be strong about it but I could tell she was so upset.'

Shortly after Kath's death, George was urged by her one surviving aunt, Valerie, to have a health screening to see if she was at risk from cancer. An old friend of Kath Budge later said: 'Vanessa wasn't keen on going but I think it was made clear to her that she would be mad not to have a check-up. Anyway, she was told by a doctor that she had a much higher than normal chance of dying young from cancer and it completely knocked her sideways. I remember meeting Vanessa shortly after she heard and she was angry and confused although she said little about it and tried to put a happy spin as usual on everything, but I could see from her eyes that she was shattered and very worried.'

Beneath that charming exterior George was in a sense very bitter about 'inheriting' the cancer gene. Kath's old friend continued: 'It particularly grated with Vanessa because she had got on so badly with Kath before she died and she was convinced in her own twisted way that her family had "given" her the cancer gene to ruin her life.'

Kath's death shocked George more than she cared to admit. Kath's old friend asked: 'Who knows if Vanessa was heartbroken when Kath died? I know that part of the reason behind that argument was that Vanessa wanted Kath to give her some more money and Kath refused. Just before she died, Vanessa had started taking Kath out for drives again and they'd go to the harbour and watch the boats coming in. This time there was no rowing about petrol money and stuff like that. I think that made Kath very happy but then she realized that Vanessa was only doing it in the hope she could get some more money off Kath. That's when they had yet another row and Vanessa said she wouldn't go to Kath's funeral. It was only then that Kath realized Vanessa was just being nice to her to make sure she left her something in her will.'

The fallout from Kath and George's bad relationship continued after her grandmother's death. Kath's old friend recalled: 'Vanessa was deliberately left out of the will by Kathleen. Only Vanessa's girls got some money. Vanessa must have been furious but ultimately Kath was right. Vanessa was a greedy, cruel, heartless person.'

Friends and members of the Budge family have speculated that George was in many ways a mirror image of her grandmother and that was why the two had such a volatile relationship. According to one relative: 'Kath and Vanessa both didn't suffer fools and had sharp tongues. They also were quite overweight and sometimes it felt as if Vanessa blamed Kath for her weight problems and that made their relationship even more strained.'

Towards the end of her life, Kath Budge lost an enormous amount of weight because of her two bouts of cancer and one relative says that in a twisted way even that weight loss irritated George: 'It was almost as if Vanessa was jealous of Kath for losing the weight because she was so clearly desperate to lose weight herself but just couldn't stop herself from eating huge quantities and piling on the pounds.'

In George's twisted mind, having cancer had certain advantages because it helped you lose weight. Ironically, she piled on even more weight in the months following her grandmother's death in 2007.

But it was the results of those cancer tests which seem

to have been the tipping point for George. One relative later said: 'Vanessa was in a sense facing a death sentence. She really did seem to change as a person from the moment she got the results of that cancer test. It's almost as if she just decided she didn't care about anything or anyone because no one had ever cared about her and protected her from bad things, like cancer.'

George had faced two pivotal moments in her life over the previous couple of years; she'd discovered she had the cancer gene and she had passed the age her mother had been when she died. Now she genuinely feared that she was destined for the same fate as her mother and sisters, as well as her grandmother.

Others who knew George at this time also insist there was a marked change in her character and attitude towards other people. One said: 'She seemed to get much harder, virtually overnight. You could see it in her face.'

George's daughters Pearl, now thirteen, and Grace, eleven, began to be left much more to their own devices. George seemed to become more distant from them and her husband Andrew. She started to lose interest in keeping the house clean and tidy. Dishes stacked up and supper often consisted of something straight out of a packet.

George had long since found it easier to emotionally detach herself because then she wouldn't be so sad and disappointed if and when someone she loved died. But this time she was the one facing a death sentence. Now that feeling of being neglected and not cared for was manifesting itself in an inner hardness. It was like a second skin of toughness that she – who had really not given a damn about anyone other than herself for years – had long since decided would enable her to do anything she pleased. After all, she might not be alive for much longer so she might as well go for it.

The new, more detached George would do whatever took her fancy. If she wanted to have more affairs with other men then so be it. She'd had that one brief fling with a man in 1996 but that had been nothing more than a fleeting extramarital relationship. Now her attitude was 'You only live once.' In fact, many who knew her at that time noted that it had become one of her favourite phrases.

Often when she was chatting away to mothers and other staff members at Little Ted's nursery where she worked she'd end the conversation by saying: 'You only live once.' Now she was going to prove that once and for all.

However, her ability to lure men into relationships would have to overcome the not inconsiderable problem of her weight. She was close to eighteen stone, which meant that she knew her appearance was unlikely to attract any new men in the local pub or when she was out shopping. She'd quite fancied some of the fathers at Little Ted's nursery, but none of them had shown much interest in her so she came up with a plan.

George created a little cubby-hole just off the main sitting room of the family house in Douglass Road and set up her computer there. She'd start to turn herself into a fully fledged cyber-mistress, a woman clever enough to use words to try and lure men into her life. She'd read all about many such relationships in the papers and weekly gossip magazines and seen loads of programmes about cyber-love on the TV.

Just as her interest in the paranormal had been fuelled by television, so she was about to embark on a completely new 'adventure' that everyone on the television seemed to be doing. So why couldn't she have a go at it? She had spent much of the previous few years glued to the telly and it seemed to inspire her to chase after a whole new, disturbing set of dreams.

PART THREE
The Evil Within

'Battle not with monsters lest ye become a monster and
if you gaze into the abyss the abyss gazes into you.'

Friedrich Nietzsche

6

Vanessa George aimed to break up the tedium and monotony of her domestic life and do some reckless, crazy things. She'd grown bored of her husband. He was certainly a good man but George wanted something more edgy. She'd never been afraid of a 'hit' of danger and now she wanted to get herself a steady, never-ending supply of it. And this way no one but her would know what she was up to so she wouldn't even be risking losing her family.

In her own strange, deluded mind, George believed her family were lucky to have her. She was a good, caring mother. She had a worthwhile job in a nursery where she was immensely popular so why shouldn't she have a bit of fun on the side? It wouldn't harm anyone this way, would it? Caring about people only ever led to bitter disappointments. This way, she really could have her cake *and* eat it.

So one weekend not long after her Granny Kath's death from cancer, Vanessa George renamed herself 'Vee George' on the internet and joined the social networking site Facebook with the sole intention of finding herself a 'playmate'. She was already known as 'Vee' at work. She rather liked the sound of 'Vee'. It made her feel a little more exotic.

George – already with a reputation for being very greedy when it came to food – was intending to gorge herself on a few sick and twisted men. Surely they would be a bit more fun than her boring old life back in Douglass Road, Plymouth?

Like hundreds of millions of others worldwide, 'Vee George' enjoyed exploring all the different applications available on the Facebook site like sending cyber-drinks and gifts to her friends. One of her favourite applications was 'Are You Interested?', a programme in which users who requested the application were sent photos of random singletons of the opposite sex and encouraged to click 'yes' or 'no', depending on whether the picture took their fancy. They could also find out who'd clicked 'yes' to them and even send messages to find out more about them.

Whatever motivated George to betray her marriage vows that first time ten years earlier clearly didn't get completely out of her system. She was soon talking openly to her workmates at Little Ted's nursery about other men she was 'meeting' on the internet. They were surprised about how open she was but that was Vee to a T. The huge, over-suntanned lady with the ever-beaming smile was a walking contradiction in many ways. But underneath it all she seemed to have a heart of gold so what did it matter if she indulged herself in a few harmless fantasy friends on the internet?

Soon she was spending increasingly long amounts of time on the computer, which she had now very carefully positioned in that open cubby-hole directly off the living room. While Andrew and the girls sat watching the telly just a few feet away, George would be 'chatting' online to men she met in internet chat rooms or on social networking sites like Facebook.

On Facebook, George – described by other members as the 'life and soul of the party' – even posted pictures of herself with a plastic moustache from a Christmas cracker stuck on her forehead just to keep up that happy-go-lucky image which she enjoyed amongst the other staff members at Little Ted's.

With her back to her family in the lounge, she upped the time she'd spend online to the point where it seemed that every spare moment was spent flirting with her new internet acquaintances. And she continued to boast about them to colleagues at the nursery. Her online banter became increasingly sexually explicit and she talked openly about being in the market for 'no-strings fun'. She took graphic photos of herself with her mobile phone and sent them to men she encountered online. One man who 'met' her on Facebook later told the *Sun*: 'She was up for anything.'

It's unclear how many of these online encounters, if any, went on to be enacted in real life. Certainly George would give friends and work colleagues the impression of a rampant sex life full of illicit trysts in hotels, but she would later claim in a letter to her husband that there had only been one such meeting.

'The only bloke I did meet was the one from Ford,' she wrote. 'We met up a couple of times, nothing in it, just some fun.'

That phrase 'just some fun' seemed to be the key to George's attitude when she first started trawling the internet for men. In her mind this was all harmless stuff. She even felt in a twisted way that she deserved it because she'd been so 'well-behaved' for so many years during her marriage, apart from that brief affair back in 1996.

Not surprisingly, George and her husband Andrew's marriage gradually began to buckle as her obsession with the internet grew. At home, her housework ground to a virtual halt. Surfaces gathered more and more dust and pans remained unwashed as she neglected chores in favour of grabbing every precious moment online. Her daughters too continued to be even more overlooked as George's attention was taken up almost entirely with her cyber-activities. Where once she would be around when the girls came home from school, waiting to hear bits of news from their day, now more often she was glued to the computer screen when they walked in. Uniforms were frequently unwashed, packed lunches unmade. Dinners were always frozen meals, hastily shoved into the oven and often left to burn while she sat transfixed by what was happening online. Other times neighbours would see her sitting out on her doorstep hunched over her mobile phone, furiously texting.

Because the cubby-hole was so compact, George couldn't close it off, but instead she angled the glass door so that it would reflect what was happening in the room behind her. If she saw someone getting up, she'd immediate flick from whatever she was doing so that by the time they walked past she'd have something innocuous up on-screen – a news page or her Facebook page. On the rare occasions she was so engrossed she didn't notice someone behind her, she'd become incensed, demanding to know what they wanted and what they were doing.

She and her husband started leading semi-separate lives, going to bed at different times, although bizarrely George initiated sex with her husband even more often as her online 'sexcapades' deepened.

And yet, while life at home was starting to unravel, at work George remained the same popular, ebullient figure she'd always been, quick to offer help if a child needed changing or taking to the toilet. Often parents would come to pick up their children and be handed a bag of wet clothes by the smiling nursery worker. 'Had another accident, I'm afraid.'

Like many who worked in childcare, George would frequently undergo training to keep up with the new guidelines that seemed to be constantly being issued by the Government. In 2008 she did a course on how to spot early signs of sexual abuse. It was a subject outspoken Vee George felt particularly strongly about. If ever an item about a paedophile came on the television news, she'd leap to her feet swearing at the screen and shouting: 'Fucking bastard, cut his fucking balls off.' She'd even joined a Facebook group called Against Child Abuse, adding her name and photo to the site, which had 300,000 members worldwide.

George also continued to tear herself away from her beloved computer for nights out with nursery parents and staff. You could always depend on friendly Vee to play the fool and she was always in demand for any social outings. At times it seemed as if even being at work was an extension of George's social life. The staff all knew each other so well there was often a real party atmosphere at Little Ted's.

Later, of course, some parents would question whether the closeness of the staff might have led to a relaxing of normally stringent nursery regulations.

Though they'd got used to Vee's talk about meeting strange men, at one stage colleagues began noticing she was mentioning one man more than the others – Colin Blanchard. Soon he was pretty much all she talked about.

'She just said he was a businessman with money,' said a former colleague, Lynn Newcombe, who described how George planned a whole new life with Blanchard. 'She was totally besotted with him and said, "We are going to run away together." We thought it was just another of her fantasies.'

Unfortunately Colin Blanchard would turn out to be all too terrifyingly real.

It was through Facebook – the world's most popular social networking website used by over 300 million people – that George met the man who would become her obsession.

As usual, she was spending her evenings emailing men she already knew and idly flicking through links on her Facebook page. When the photo of Colin Blanchard flashed up on the 'Are You Interested?' application at the end of December 2008, there was something about the big man with the close-shaven head and deep-set eyes that took her fancy.

Hmmm . . . he's nice-looking, she thought, clicking on the 'yes' option.

Before long she had a message back – just the usual polite chit-chat. 'Hi, how are you?' Blanchard had written unoriginally. 'Have you had a nice day'?

The two exchanged a few messages and confirmed each other as Facebook friends so that each could access the other's personal Facebook page and send private messages. More messages were exchanged and then Blanchard asked: 'Do you have an MSN account?'

Despite all those long hours spent on the internet, George hadn't got round to setting up an instant messaging account where you can chat with someone online in real time instead of sending whole messages back and forth. It was a matter of minutes to set up an account and before long the two strangers were chatting regularly online, shedding inhibitions as they went. Blanchard, it turned out, was also married. He lived in Rochdale, some 250 miles from Plymouth, with his wife and daughter and was clearly doing very well as a businessman. As with most of George's online encounters, talk soon turned to sex.

'Tell me your fantasies,' Blanchard urged her in one conversation. This was George's favourite kind of chat and she indulged her imagination, inventing outlandish scenarios. Blanchard joined in, propelling the conversation on until out of the blue he dropped in that he'd been abused as a child.

'Oh that's awful,' typed George.

'No, it was really nice,' came the unexpected reply.

George was taken aback. *Oh, my goodness. I've a kinky one here . . .*

Incredibly, instead of running a mile after Blanchard's disturbing revelation, the nursery worker not only continued chatting but actually, in her own words, 'played along' with Blanchard.

Her new penpal needed little encouragement to open up about his own warped fantasies, starting with his own experiences of being abused as a child, which seemed to have kick-started a lifelong obsession. With every new message, Blanchard's fantasies became bolder and ever more extreme.

George – or 'daddys_princess69' as she now called herself on her new Hotmail account – could have stopped him at any time. She could have done any number of things, changed the subject, stopped answering his messages, blocked him from her friends list.

She did none of those things. Whether because she was already infatuated with Blanchard and couldn't bear to do anything to disappoint him, or because the horrible fantasies he began detailing to her in some way triggered corresponding fantasies of her own, no one can be sure. All that is clear is that Vanessa George, respectable mother of two, trusted nursery worker, life and soul of the party, willingly entered into an online correspondence with a man she'd never met in which the abuse of children became a recurring topic.

At work, while she was careful not to drop any hints about her new friend's predilections, she talked about 'Colin' more and more. He was a well-off businessman, she told her friends proudly. She couldn't wait to meet him.

Blanchard, aware by this time that George worked in a nursery and therefore had, to his eyes, unlimited access to what he most craved, did everything he could to encourage her adulation. 'I want you in my life,' he'd tell her. 'I've told my mum about you.'

The two started talking several times a day, using texts, emails and even webcams. George bought a second, secret mobile phone, which she called her 'fun phone' and used to text Blanchard and to send him the graphic sexual images she took of herself. They discussed meeting up, even running away together. George, hugely overweight, bored, approaching forty, soaked up the attention and in return she willingly gave Blanchard what he so obviously wanted, her own fantasies, each one more twisted than the one before, many also involving children and abuse, knowing that the reward for letting her imagination run free was his approval.

When Blanchard took things to the next level, suggesting she take photos of the children in her charge, it was another obvious point where the hitherto law-abiding childcare worker could have pulled out of the relationship, realizing it was about to cross an essential line that would place her outside everything that she'd known up until that point. It was the last point at which she could have walked away. Yet she did not.

'What would you do for me if I did something like that?' she asked instead, as if Blanchard had asked her for a lift home or for a job reference rather than to take photographs of the 'parts' of babies entrusted to her care, knowing full well that photography of any kind was expressly prohibited within the nursery.

Did she have doubts that first day as she sneaked her 'fun phone' into the toilets with her when she took a little girl for nappy-changing? Did her finger hover uncertainly over the select key before she clicked to take the first of what would be a sickeningly long series of pornographic photographs?

It seems no one will ever fully know what went on in the nursery worker's head, but when she came back from the toilets, her tiny charge freshly changed, George had crossed that invisible, but undisguisable line. There would be no going back.

7

So what of Colin Blanchard, the man who'd brought about this sea-change in the life of this previously unremarkable middle-aged woman?

Like George, Colin Blanchard was born in 1970. He grew up in the tough Norris Green area of Liverpool, attending schools in the area and in north Liverpool – Ranworth Square primary school and then Anfield Comprehensive.

Blanchard was always one for having big ideas, usually with little basis in reality. He wanted the nicer things in life, the flash cars, the big houses, but all that frustratingly seemed a world away when he started his working life in Knowsley, Merseyside. He was employed by Knowsley Community College at the start of 1994 as a 'home-based trainer', working for an arm of the college called Knowsley Consultants.

In August 1994, after only six months in the job, he was sacked while still in his probationary period. According to the college's vice-principal, John Oakes: 'Blanchard was supposed to attend his disciplinary meeting, but he never showed up. There were a number of issues related to concern about his performance of work.' The college scrutinized his files, and it seems unlikely he worked directly with children during his short period there.

After that Blanchard decided entrepreneurialism was the

way forward and began a pattern of setting up short-lived computer and IT-based businesses, most of which ended badly. However, with a friend, Mike Longson, he built up a computer business called Empire Computers in Ashton-under-Lyne in the late 1990s. The business did well and the pair sold it reportedly for a six-figure sum.

Blanchard and his wife Anne first moved onto a new executive housing development just off Smithy Bridge Street, Littleborough, near Rochdale in Lancashire, shortly after it was completed in the summer of 2000. To their neighbours Richard and Susan Parker they seemed like a nice couple at first. 'Colin and Anne were the second people to move here after us. He seemed a friendly enough chap and there was certainly no hint of what was to come many years later,' recalled Richard Parker.

Within months, Blanchard's business partner, Mike Longson, and his wife Sue had moved in next door to Blanchard. 'They were very close friends,' observed Parker. 'They did everything together. They even had the same huge conservatories built at the back of the house, which cost an absolute fortune.'

Blanchard and Mike Longson also had identical palm trees delivered into their back gardens by a crane, which swung them over the roof of each house. 'Those huge trees must have cost many thousands of pounds and then they had them both removed because they nearly died in the cold climate and they were then replaced by weeping willows,' recalled Richard Parker.

To his neighbours and friends, Colin Blanchard seemed

to be rolling in cash. He wore a leather jacket and had his jeans well pressed and always maintained a very closely cropped hairstyle. As one resident on the close pointed out: 'At best he was a Scouser scallywag, at worst he was a major criminal face. He certainly played that part of being a villain to perfection.'

Meanwhile Blanchard continued to spend money like water. According to his neighbour: 'It was almost as if they needed to spend it all as quickly as possible. There were always loads of different cars – some high spec, some not – in the driveway. I know criminals often change cars so it did make a lot of us here think twice about what he was really up to.'

Richard and Susan Parker also soon noticed that Blanchard's influx of cash seemed to come in waves. Richard Parker commented: 'When Colin was flush he paid cash for everything and there was no doubt that he did behave like a criminal and we all wondered where he really made his money.'

Then about two years after he had moved into his house, the police and Customs officers raided Blanchard's home because he was suspected of a VAT fraud. Blanchard was alleged to have been selling electrical goods from abroad and not paying any VAT on them. Blanchard's computers were searched as part of the Customs and Excise VAT fraud investigation. A number of images of child pornography were found.

Though Blanchard would later claim the images were there when he bought the computer, he was given a police caution and placed on the sex offenders register for five years. He was also banned from being a company director until 2020. Throughout those five years, he would be subject to monitoring from the sex offenders management unit at Greater Manchester Police, including home visits and having to notify officers if he moved or went away from home for prolonged periods.

Around the time of Blanchard's first caution for possessing child pornography, Richard Parker bumped into him in the street outside his house. 'It was strange because he made a point of telling me how he had bought all these secondhand computers and they had all this vile porn on them. It was as if he was trying to build up an alibi. He even said to me: "I didn't realize there was all this stuff on the computers." He was obviously covering his tracks.'

None of Blanchard's neighbours had any idea that he had already been cautioned about the child porn. It wasn't until more than five years later that it was even revealed that Blanchard had been put on the sex offenders register. He was only on the register for five years because he had been cautioned, not actually arrested and charged by police.

Looking back, Richard Parker is deeply disturbed by something else Blanchard did around this time: 'I kept bumping into Colin in the street and he was forever offering to baby-sit our children.' The Parkers are professional foster parents and Richard Parker is horrified at the thought of what might have happened if he had taken up Blanchard's offer. 'Colin was a very affable guy and he seemed to genuinely care about children, especially when he first moved here before he had a child of his own with Anne. He also used to talk to the other neighbours and offer them his baby-sitting services. We are foster carers for very young children and we obviously never had any idea he was involved in paedophilia.'

Today Richard and Susan Parker are wracked with concern that Blanchard might also have been secretly filming their foster children from his house just fifteen yards away. 'I keep wondering if he was filming the children. It's a horrible thing to contemplate,' added Richard.

The Parkers are still angry that no one informed them of Blanchard's status on the child sex register, which was set up precisely for that purpose. Richard Parker also says that Blanchard was so controlling towards his wife that he called her Anne-Marie rather than Anne. 'I don't know why he did that but it tells you a lot about the man. Anne's family were hardly ever around at the house before all this happened. Apparently he had banned her from having anything to do with the family.'

Across the road from Blanchard's detached home, another resident, Kevin, a computer expert, was typical of those, including dentists, accountants and builders, who lived on this very desirable estate. He revealed that Blanchard also offered his baby-sitting services to him and his family. 'I was chilled to the bone when I later realized what his reasons might have been.'

Blanchard admitted to his neighbour Kevin that he had bought and sold cars in the past. Kevin added: 'Colin was a Liverpool scallywag and a ducker and a diver. His strong Scouser accent made him sound even more dodgy.'

But Colin Blanchard certainly wasn't easy-going with *all* his neighbours. He had a run-in with one neighbour who bred Dobermans and Blanchard complained about the barking of his dogs. But as Richard Parker later said: 'Yet we never even heard them.'

Mr Parker did recall that the dog Blanchard was later accused of sexually abusing was 'a really unhappy dog that would yap on all the time. He also had an Alsatian at one stage. But they never took him out for walks.'

Colin Blanchard always seemed very pleased with himself back in the early days when he resided on that 'posh' estate, near Rochdale. He appeared to be living up to his own inflated image of himself. In a sense he was living a dream. He'd married twice, both times in his twenties. Now he and his second wife, Anne, were living in a four-bedroomed detached house on a recently built executive housing estate overlooking open countryside. It couldn't get much better than that, surely?

Blanchard continued to boast to his neighbours about how well he'd done for himself. Yet most of his claims were fabrications – he told of ferrying Liverpool football players around on his private jet, making movies and having millions in cash stashed away in Dubai. He posted photographs of his Aston Martin DB9 on the net, omitting to mention that it was hired.

One neighbour attended a party at Blanchard's house and came home with a new nickname for Blanchard: ' "Billy Bullshit", because he could blag for Britain. Blanchard even insisted he still had millions of pounds stashed away in Dubai,' recalled that neighbour.

When a couple of other neighbours turned down

Blanchard's offer of baby-sitting, it wasn't because of any sinister suspicions but because they considered him a fantasist with a tenuous grip on reality and 'he was hardly the sort of person you'd hire as a baby-sitter,' explained one neighbour.

The Parkers, as well as many other residents in the small cul-de-sac, soon learned from Blanchard and his wife Anne that they had been on IVF treatment for years in a bid to be parents. 'They'd been married for quite a long time and I think they got pretty desperate to have a child,' said Richard Parker.

Meanwhile, Blanchard and his next-door neighbour and business partner Mike Longson continued to be close friends. Blanchard was even best man at Longson's wedding, although their friendship would eventually end in business catastrophe and acrimony between the two men. Their row was so serious that Mike Longson and his wife Sue ended up moving out of their expensively decorated detached house next door to Blanchard and onto a caravan site on nearby Hollingworth Lake. Mike Longson later told associates he would never have anything to do with Blanchard ever again.

Back on the quiet estate, neighbours began noticing some strange behaviour at Blanchard's house. Richard Parker observed: 'Very rarely did we ever see women at the house. It was nearly always men and there seemed to be loads of them at any given time.'

Police investigators probing Blanchard's activities have dismissed claims that Blanchard had set up some kind of business buying and selling pornographic images of underage children. But if neighbours are to be believed then it does seem that Blanchard was hosting some very unusual 'gatherings' at the house, lived in only by his vulnerable wife and later their very young child, plus that dog Blanchard would later be prosecuted for sexually abusing.

When Blanchard wasn't wearing his familiar black leather jacket and jeans he could be seen in shorts, even in the middle of winter. 'That was typical Colin, trying to prove he was some tough macho guy,' commented one neighbour.

Blanchard was without doubt a charming, gregarious character. He even became close friends with his local window cleaner, who used to spend long periods of time helping Blanchard move furniture around. Blanchard even lent the window cleaner his car and at Christmas the same man would put up all the fairy lights outside Blanchard's house. 'They were always the most expensive and usually put the rest of us to shame,' said one neighbour.

In every room of Blanchard's mansion there were vast plasma screen TV sets plus a huge collection of books on true crime and criminology. As one neighbour speculated: 'That makes him sound even more like a real criminal. Why would he bother with those books if he wasn't?'

By the middle of 2005 the numerous visible trappings of wealth in Blanchard's modern home also included a den kitted out with computer equipment where he worked on his 'deals'. There were also a brand-new Volvo in the drive and leather sofas indoors, not to mention the weeping willow tree which had replaced the palm tree that had wilted and been hoisted out of the garden again by crane.

On Friends Reunited, Blanchard boasted : 'I'm living the

dream in sunny, I wish, Lancashire, enjoying work. My granddad passed away recently and I visited Norris Green again for first time in years. Simply couldn't believe it was the same place I grew up in, what happened? Just sold a company and am now splitting my time working in advertising and movies.'

To his neighbours, Colin Blanchard continued playing the big-shot businessman. Even more men came and went in cars with blacked-out windows. He could often be seen doing business deals on his mobile, pacing up and down the path outside his home.

In reality, however, business was anything but booming. The second company he'd set up with Mike Longson, an internet café and computer company called Computer Bay in Dukinfield, Greater Manchester, had long since gone bust, leaving a trail of debts. Longson later complained: 'I wish that I had never met Colin. He seems to have caused misery to everyone.'

Patrick McIntosh was poached from a computer game shop to manage that last venture involving Blanchard and Mike Longson. The business did very well initially and then Customs and Excise came knocking once again. 'That was the beginning of the end. We never saw Colin after that,' remembered Mr McIntosh. 'The money ran out. We couldn't pay the staff and the place closed down.'

The failure of Computer Bay didn't put Colin Blanchard off the entrepreneurial route he was determined would one day bring him even more wealth than he already claimed as his own. So he simply relocated his centre of operations to Trafford Park, Manchester, still giving every impression of being a successful businessman with money behind him.

Again, as so often with Colin Blanchard, the outward appearance belied a very different reality. Though he acted like a well-heeled business tycoon, Blanchard was actually deep in debt – and getting deeper by the day.

But his finances weren't the worst of Blanchard's troubles. The high-living Liverpudlian was still nursing a far more disturbing secret.

To his latest business partners, with whom he now worked in a company buying and selling IT equipment in Trafford Park, Blanchard only mentioned he'd been the subject of that VAT fraud investigation which was still having repercussions. They knew better than to question him further as Blanchard had a reputation for being economical with the truth.

One former business associate remarked: 'He'd sell his own mother if he could. He liked to think he was a gangster and said he was a friend of the Noonan crime family in Manchester.'

What helped Blanchard get away with his lies was his likeability. A local Asian businessman and former partner, Noman Ahmed, who knew him on and off for ten years, explained: 'He was a compulsive liar. I know he lied and to be honest he was a struggle to do business with sometimes. But I liked him. He had the right contacts. He knew a lot of heavy people – politicians, businessmen, celebs.

'He was very well-connected, which made him a good businessman. And he was a great blagger. He'd get into something to prove that he could get it for you, no matter how difficult it was. It's his character, almost as if he was showing off what he could get or get people to do for him.'

Ahmed recalled the Blanchards being thrilled at the birth of their daughter after years of trying for a family. 'She was a miracle child for them.'

The little girl's room was soon filled with expensive toys and for a while she attended a private nursery, even though Anne Blanchard didn't work.

Back on that exclusive estate where Blanchard and his family lived, his neighbour Richard Parker saw that 'Colin was very controlling while his wife Anne seemed much more fragile. They always did everything together. They even took the child to nursery together, even though she often drove. It was almost as if he was constantly keeping an eye on her in case something happened.'

The Parkers also noticed that following the birth of Blanchard's daughter in 2004 the child was rarely seen. 'They got much more isolated and we hardly ever saw them. After a private nursery the little girl went to the local St Andrew's primary school, although that seemed strange because there was a nearer one they could have sent her to,' Richard Parker said, and he believes that around this time – 2006/7 – Blanchard must have been starting to run short of money. 'I guess that must be why he switched the little girl from a fee-paying school to a local one,' he added.

But it was the physical appearance of Blanchard's wife which aroused the most concern. As Parker described her: 'Anne was late thirties, early forties and she looked about sixty. It was as if she had the cares of the whole world on her shoulders.'

The only time Anne Blanchard did manage to escape

her husband's attentions was on some Saturday mornings. Richard Parker said that 'She'd put the baby in the car and disappear. Goodness knows where she was going but she'd be gone for at least half the day.'

Another neighbour recalled that one time the Blanchards had what they described as a children's party. 'But it actually turned out to be a thank you to the people who laid the grass in his garden. He got in a huge order from McDonald's for that one. Typical Colin.'

And other neighbours also noticed the fragile state of Blanchard's long-suffering wife. 'She looked so sad and tired. She looked haunted.'

Meanwhile more men continued visiting the Blanchards' detached house, which has stuck in so many other neighbours' minds since Blanchard's arrest. One said: 'I remember thinking it was strange because there were simply no women ever going in there.'

A neighbour who visited Blanchard to swap notes regarding a stereo system he'd just had installed commented that 'He had those massive TVs in every room. Colin seemed pleasant enough as he showed me round but the interior seemed cold and impersonal. The TVs dominated the rooms and there were hardly any personal belongings anywhere.'

Blanchard himself already had another child – a boy – by his previous wife, who still lived in his home city of Liverpool. Neighbours recall seeing the boy – in his early teens – visiting the house with his father before the birth of Blanchard's second child by his new wife, Anne. 'Colin would pick the boy up and bring him over for the weekend but we never saw him again at the house after the birth of their daughter,' remembered Richard Parker.

As with everything about Colin Blanchard, however, appearances were deceptive. Inside the house just off Smithy Bridge Road with its large conservatory, the rooms echoed with secrets. Blanchard's 'den' continued to be his exclusive kingdom. His computers were strictly out of bounds for his wife and their child. He claimed they held vital work-related information.

What they actually contained were some of the grossest images on the child pornography scale, featuring rape, incest, animals and 'extremely serious' sexual abuse of children, some barely a year old. Blanchard had even videoed himself engaged in that sex act with his pet shitzhu, Bubba.

Police who later raided Blanchard's house at the time of his arrest discovered tens of thousands of deeply disturbing images in various computers at the Blanchard family house. One local police officer explained: 'We suspect that Blanchard was into this sort of stuff long before he met Vanessa George.'

In 2008 Blanchard attempted to set up yet another new business enterprise with Noman Ahmed. 'It was typical Colin to flit from business to business,' Ahmed later recalled.

At the same time Blanchard also did a special training course in order to qualify to help people avoid paying off their credit card debts. 'That was a classic Colin move. He was an opportunist and he reckoned the recession was going to end up meaning lots of business for him,' said another associate.

Typically, Blanchard was juggling his work opportunities and was doing the same thing with the 'harem' of women he sent graphic emails to. 'He was the ultimate ducker and diver. In some ways he couldn't help himself. He was addicted to it. I suppose it was a power thing in a way' was the opinion of one former associate.

Blanchard was spending increasing amounts of time on the internet with a 'posse' of women he'd 'seduced' through emails and messages and texts. He was by this stage openly nurturing some of these women by exchanging appalling underage pornographic images. And to most of these women he seems to have professed his undying love. It was a perfect platform for a cold predator to try and 'turn' a bunch of lonely women into willing accomplices.

While Blanchard's friends and business partners had no idea of his true nature, he had no such compunctions about sharing the contents of his imagination and hard drive with his new Facebook friend in Plymouth, Vee George, after they first started talking in December 2008. As their cyber-relationship developed, he sent her images of himself abusing children and she reciprocated with photographs taken of the children in her care.

Was she aware of just how heinous a crime she was committing? Did she, as she'd later claim, feel 'disgusted' with herself at the 'vile' things she was doing? It's unlikely we'll ever know for sure.

What we do know is that she soon realized that the more graphic the photos she took, the more grateful Blanchard appeared, and the more attention he showered upon her.

Soon they were exchanging up to fifty-five images, texts and calls a day. This was no longer a temporary blip in her real life; it was fast becoming reality itself.

Blanchard declared his love for Vee and the besotted George allowed herself to imagine how wonderful life would be when they'd run away together. But despite her romantic fantasies, she knew that it was her position as a nursery worker with ready access to small children which gave her the most bargaining power in the relationship. Desperate to engineer a meeting with the object of her desires, she would use her position to try to persuade Blanchard to turn up 'in the flesh'.

One mobile exchange later recaptured by police demonstrates how she pandered to his fantasies, bartering her 'services' in exchange for promises of commitment.

CB: I want pics of them asleep . . . Get them drugged n take pics of them asleep

VG: When ive met you properly then I'll do things like that ok xxx

CB: Ok x x x x

But to her increasing frustration, any attempts to lure Blanchard into a physical 'real life' encounter ended in failure. She even went as far as arranging a tryst at a Premier Inn in Rochdale, booking the room on her husband's credit card, only for her internet lover to fail to turn up. She then contacted another man she had met online and had sex with him at the hotel instead.

Yet her obsession with Blanchard continued to grow

and she became increasingly desperate to please him, typing out long and ever more depraved fantasies she knew would get his attention. She even started talking about kidnapping a child. Spotting a little boy waiting for his mum outside a toilet cubicle at Plymouth railway station, she texted Blanchard: 'That would have been the perfect opportunity to snatch him, wouldn't it?'

At Little Ted's, personal phones were not allowed and George was even once told off for having one. But rules were 'relaxed' because the in-house phone was unreliable. And then of course the eighteen-stone George had bought herself that second, secret mobile telephone, which she referred to as her 'fun phone' or 'dirty phone'. She kept it hidden in her expansive cleavage so she could furtively look down at her chest to check for indecent messages.

At one stage she was in contact with up to fifteen men at a time and continued to boast of her extramarital sexual exploits to friends – who said she acted 'like a bitch on heat'. These included engaging in oral sex with a stranger on moorland near her home for which she claimed she received money. She also offered her services to a mechanic in exchange for work carried out on her car.

At the nursery, George would take indecent photographs of children and then send Blanchard a text message informing him that images were on their way. 'Two more pics for you baby,' she wrote on one occasion, signing off: 'Your paedo whore mumma'. George was becoming increasingly obsessed with sex and commented to one child's father at the nursery that his boy was 'well-endowed'.

*

In the spring of 2009 George went with her daughters to their holiday caravan in Cornwall. Her husband Andrew couldn't make it because he was working. Within minutes of them arriving at the caravan, George was poring over her laptop and making mobile calls and sending texts. When Pearl and Grace went off to join in with caravan holiday activities, George found herself gazing across the park where the children ran around playing unattended and wandered casually in and out of the toilet block. It was the kind of friendly site where parents felt able to relax their grip and give their kids the kind of freedom they might normally be denied.

What no one knew at that time was that George was already eyeing up children playing at the caravan park while she was 'talking' by email with that man called Colin. In one chilling message she wrote: 'My God, there are so many children running loose round here I could grab one no problem at all. And we could get a room in the Premier Inn.'

Then she added: 'God, this is like a goldmine here, there are so many children running free, no immediate parent around, easily one could go missing.' On another occasion during the same break at the caravan park, George sent Blanchard a message after spotting a little boy as he waited for his mum outside a lavatory cubicle and entertained the same kidnapping fantasy as she had at Plymouth railway station.

As George's fantasies grew more extreme, her need for reassurance from Blanchard also increased. 'Can you see a future for us?' she'd pressure him. 'Yes, definitely,' would come the reply.

But George could never feel fully secure, because as she was getting more and more deeply involved with Blanchard, she'd made a painful discovery.

Blanchard told George he had found another woman, whom he described as being 'really dirty, filthy'.

She had a love rival.

8

The 'other woman' in Blanchard's cyber-life was Angela Allen, a 39-year-old mother of two from Nottingham. While George and Colin Blanchard hid their crimes behind a veneer of respectability, Allen had no such pretensions.

She'd been brought up in a long succession of care homes where, according to fellow resident Jerry Coyne, forty-four, who wrote a book about the cruelty he suffered at the notorious Nazareth House in Nottingham: 'She loved to watch while the nuns abused the other kids. She was a very odd child.'

These days home was a squalid flat housed within a pebbledashed house in Nine Acre Gardens, in the rundown Nottingham suburb of Bulwell. Despite being a single mother to her two small daughters, aged two and four, Allen made little attempt to make the flat into any kind of home. The place was filthy and there was little in the way of furniture or food.

As a younger woman, Allen had spent years working as a prostitute in Manchester. As well as appearing before the courts on six occasions on charges of soliciting, she was convicted of theft in 1992. Those charges were enough to scupper her brief career working in a bank.

She was now living on benefits, and neighbours, who described Allen as 'loud and aggressive', reported that since her ex-partner, a traffic warden, had moved out, the flat had become a magnet for young men and teenage boys. Police would later describe Allen as living on the 'fringe of society' and it seems clear she didn't give much thought to what other people thought of her or how she was judged.

Allen's Facebook page – accompanied by a picture of a hand pushing down into a pair of red knickers – left little doubt that she was obsessed with sex. Alongside photographs that showed her scantily dressed, she boasted about thinking of sex '95 per cent of the time'. Just the kind of woman Blanchard was looking for.

In the autumn of 2008, Angela Allen and Colin Blanchard became Facebook friends and soon began to send each other increasingly explicit text messages, emails and pictures.

'Ang Bank', as she styled herself on the web, presumably in reference to her brief and ignominious banking career, didn't have to be persuaded to share her most basic fantasies. If anything, she was even more extreme than Blanchard, talking happily about incest, rape of children and sex with animals.

Allen, like George, became infatuated with Colin Blanchard, going on to swap 1,500 images with him of children being abused, and there's some speculation that she also tried to instigate a face-to-face meeting in December 2008.

Not long afterwards, Blanchard told her about his new online conquest, quick to emphasize the advantages offered by Vee George's line of work. He introduced the two women to one another online and in doing so forged the triangle of abuse and depravity that would eventually shock the nation.

Allen and George – now fully aware of each other's existence – began to compete for Colin Blanchard's affections and approval, each viewing the other as a rival. It became a point of pride as to who could supply the best pictures for Blanchard's satisfaction.

Both women would send graphic images of themselves to Blanchard and they'd indulge in three-way video conferences where, thanks to webcams on their personal computers, they could 'perform' for each other. Later police would uncover evidence that Blanchard and Allen even broadcast some of their abuse 'live' in this way.

Colleagues at Little Ted's nursery were shocked by the way that George seemed to only have one thing on her mind at work and even fantasized about the children's dads. A workmate, Isaura Coburn, explained: 'When I started at Little Ted's, she had been there for a few months. She was bubbly and fun-loving, but could be very loud and a bit pushy. She tended to work more in the baby room, and if we were in there we would get chatting. Her favourite topic of conversation by far was sex. It was like it was the only thing on her mind and her life revolved around it. She had a really dirty mind and if there was a good-looking guy in the paper she'd always say something like, "I'd love to do him", or "I'd love to f*** him." She always swore a lot at work, even though she was surrounded by children. She would make comments about some of the parents, saying she would love to have sex with the dads.

'She contacted some of them on Facebook and sent them flirty messages as well ... we all just saw it as an extension of her sociable personality. When she talked about sex we assumed she meant with her husband, but she hinted that she'd had an affair about twelve years ago.'

Isaura added: 'Everyone knew she spent loads of her free time on the internet. I first heard about Blanchard at the beginning of the year when she began talking about this tall, dark, handsome man she had met online. We knew that she was texting him and she was always saying how she couldn't wait to get home to talk to him online. She showed us a picture of his face he had sent her, but she never showed us any of the texts.

'We had a fair idea they were sending each other sexual texts and pictures – but we never for one remote second imagined it involved kids. There was one time when she was working with a younger woman and Blanchard texted, asking if she would send him a picture of the two of them together.

'Vanessa said, "What do you think?" but the other girl just said, "That's disgusting", and laughed it off. She even bought a second pay-as-you-go phone she used to contact him, which is probably why her husband never found out.

'She seemed to be infatuated with Blanchard. She talked as if she was ready to leave her husband and the girls and move up north to be with him.'

At home, George would wait for her husband and daughters to be out of the way, either out or asleep, before drawing the curtains and impatiently firing up her computer to watch the webcam footage, either live or recorded.

Angela Allen was given the number to her new friend Vee's 'fun phone' and contacted her on her daddys_ princess69@hotmail.com account. While the women mostly communicated through Blanchard, they also contacted each other directly, although they didn't engage in sexual chat directly with each other. Their email exchanges reveal that each knew exactly where the other was getting the images they'd vie with each other to send and receive.

Allen in particular seemed to have no boundaries when it came to how far she'd go to satisfy her own and Blanchard's desires. There was a notable element of one-upmanship as she detailed to the others things she'd either done or wanted to do.

On one occasion, she spoke of wanting to watch while strangers rape a three-year-old girl she regarded as her sexual 'trophy' and even issued an open invitation to strangers to participate. It was later suggested she'd spent time and effort in coaching the child to engage in acts of depravity. Online, she sent Blanchard a graphic account of one such imagined assault.

Blanchard, clearly excited by the idea, suggested that she take a specific photo. 'Mmmmmm ok,' she texted back, before reminding him that they were due to 'meet' up on the webcam later. 'But if I don't theres all ways cam 2nite.'

And all the time there was a constant undercurrent of competition between the two women, who each used a form of crude and explicit shorthand in their messages to Blanchard.

They'd describe the most sordid and explicit fantasies involving bestiality and violent abuse, before signing off: 'I love you.' And Blanchard, of course, was quick to exploit their rivalry to his own ends.

'Blanchard expressed love for each woman, and they would reciprocate,' explained Detective Inspector Tony Creely, of Greater Manchester Police's sexual crime unit. 'They would discuss sexual matters of a crude and gross nature and the abuse of children in the texts and emails.'

George knew that to hold her own in this escalating orgy of abuse, she had to play her trump card – the fact that she worked in a nursery. Since that first photo of the little girl, she'd been sending a steady stream of images to Blanchard, which he'd then send on to Allen.

On 21 April 2009 Angela Allen sent an email to Colin Blanchard showing her abusing a child, which he then sent directly on to George.

Blanchard was blatantly throwing down the gauntlet to her. It was as if he was saying to her: you want to play with the serious hitters then now is your chance. Show me what you are capable of doing. If you want my unconditional love, then you have to earn it.

George must initially have panicked. Her rival, Allen, was playing a chilling game of brinkmanship and Colin Blanchard was the ultimate prize. It seemed to George that unless she went one better then she might lose Blanchard.

Over the following few hours, her mood swung in all directions as she sat there in her cubby-hole just a few feet from her husband and two daughters. She kept studying that appalling image which Blanchard had forwarded to her and, as usual, if any of her family approached, she'd flick from that graphic photo of a child being raped to her Facebook page.

George's initial panic at the thought of 'losing' her cyber-lover Blanchard had now been replaced by a feverish state of adrenalin-fuelled excitement as she began planning her next move. That night she lay in bed next to her husband mapping out exactly how she would do it. How she would prove to Blanchard once and for all that she was his number one bitch paedo lover.

The following morning George got up, tended to her kids and then packed a couple of 'props' in her bag before setting off in her battered old blue Vauxhall for Little Ted's.

George was as merry as ever when she arrived at the nursery. In fact, staff later recalled that she seemed almost as if she was high on drugs she was so happy. One staff member said: 'Even by her standards, Vanessa seemed to be on cloud nine that morning but we were used to that so none of us took much notice.' George had hatched an appalling plan that she was about to put into action.

No one knows exactly what happened on that morning of 22 April 2009, but what is clear is that George engineered it so that she was alone with one of the toddlers in her care. She then opened up that bag and took out some 'props', including a toothbrush and a sex aid, which she used to physically abuse that child. Then she proceeded to take ten photos of the toddler. She took that number of shots because she wanted to up the ante with Blanchard. 'Ang Bank' had only managed one measly photo of that child being raped. Vee George took *ten* pictures with her camera-phone. Surely that proved she was the one for him?

Later that same day, George crammed her eighteen-stone body into that little cubby-hole back at her house. She must have been shaking with the excitement of the situation by this stage. As her two daughters played in the sitting room just a few feet away, she went into cyber-mode and carefully and clinically downloaded all ten of those repulsive images into her computer.

Her short, fat, orange-skinned fingers tingled at the tips when she tapped out Blanchard's email address. For a few moments her forefinger wavered as the cursor flickered over the 'send' sign. This was it. This was the moment when she would guarantee that he would love her for ever. He could not fail to be impressed by what she had done for him. That bitch Ang Bank could never match her.

Her brain was so focused on what she was about to do that all the noises of her children and even the smell of the burning food in the oven melted into oblivion. She only wanted one thing and she had already committed the ultimate twisted sacrifice a few hours earlier by abusing that innocent child in the nursery where she worked.

George took an enormous deep breath and then pressed on the 'send' sign and the images raced through cyberspace to Colin Blanchard's home near Rochdale, more than 250 miles away.

In Plymouth, George sat and stared at the computer screen for ages as she waited with baited breath for her cyber-lover to send back his love and gratitude.

Typically, Colin Blanchard was so 'impressed' that instead

of replying instantly to George, he forwarded all ten of those appalling images to Allen. He clearly adored cranking up the rivalry between his two 'paedo whores'. So in this way, with the bar constantly being raised, all sense of perspective and all awareness of the normal rules of society were lost.

Within days, Blanchard had 'rewarded' George for her ten obscene photographs by forwarding images of both Allen and himself violently abusing girls aged respectively three and five. Additionally the three would then send each other lengthy fantasies, many of them inspired by the images they'd seen. Over the course of six months, the trio exchanged 10,000 emails, calls and messages, with 7,000 texts being sent from George to Blanchard.

Buoyed up by how easy it had been, and by the approval she got from the others and apparently becoming herself increasingly hooked on the idea of sexual contact with children, George stepped up both the quantity of the photographs and the graphic nature. Soon the 'props' she smuggled into the nursery included more sex aids as well as that toothbrush, with which to abuse the children in her care.

This was George's currency within the triangle, which she used over and over again to try to match or better the contributions from the other two. In all she took about 150 obscene photographs of around thirty infants in her care, some as young as twelve months.

George had already acted on the initial fantasies that Blanchard encouraged by abusing those children in her care. But would she have actually taken part in some of those longer, more detailed scenarios such as snatching a child off the street or in a public toilet? While clearly most violent sexual fantasies remain just fantasies, officers who investigate predatory sex cases cite the cycle-of-offending model which explains how offenders will go through particular psychological stages, such as fantasizing about crimes before working up to the crime itself. Following the act they may go through feelings of guilt, then denial before working their way back to fantasizing all over again.

As the three-way relationship spiralled increasingly out of control, the love and approbation George had been seeking from Blanchard remained elusive. Their relationship grew more strained and difficult as George constantly pressed for reassurances, often getting back just more requests for photographs.

But, although she didn't know it yet, feeling thwarted in love was the least of her problems as the spring of 2009 passed almost imperceptibly into summer. Because, hundreds of miles away in Greater Manchester, the net was about to close in on her cyber-lover, Colin Blanchard.

9

Noman Ahmed and a handful of other businessmen worked out of a rented office based at Trafford Park business park in Manchester, a short distance from the legendary football stadium.

Ahmed had known Colin Blanchard off and on for years and, while he knew he was something of a fantasist, inventing stories of multi-million-pound business deals which were always just around the corner, he couldn't help liking the mouthy Liverpudlian. Plus Blanchard, for all his posturing, seemed to be genuinely well-connected in the area, knowing the movers and shakers around that part of Greater Manchester. Additionally, Blanchard's daughter was friendly with Ahmed's and the two would often play together.

Blanchard was known as a wheeler-dealer and would regularly pop into Ahmed's office to talk about deals he was making with the other businessmen based there. Sometimes he'd use the office facilities to make calls and arrange meetings, often borrowing Ahmed's own computer to access his own Google mail, logging in with his own address and password.

On Monday, 1 June 2009, Blanchard visited the office – as usual, using Ahmed's computer to send some important emails. But, for once, the normally computer-savvy paedophile made a critical mistake. He forgot to log out of his

Google mail on Ahmed's computer. When Ahmed tried to access his own Google mail site a few days later on Friday, 5 June, he found himself confronted with all of Blanchard's emails.

It took a few seconds to work out that this wasn't his account. Noman Ahmed had no interest in reading any of Blanchard's personal emails, but as his finger hovered over the mouse to click on 'sign out', a name in the inbox caught Ahmed's eye. It was a message from one of his own contacts in Dubai. Ahmed, who'd long harboured suspicions that Blanchard could be trying to edge him out of deals, decided to investigate.

He later explained: 'There were deals he was engaged in relating to one of my contacts in Dubai and I was interested in that. I realized he was usurping my contact, doing a deal behind my back.'

After a quick scan of Blanchard's inbox, Ahmed clicked on his 'sent' folder, looking for more evidence that his colleague was trying to double-cross him. But scrolling down the messages, he was intrigued by the numbers of photographs that Blanchard seemed to be sending out, to a variety of women recipients. Feeling slightly guilty, he double-clicked on a few and was stunned to find 'bizarre' images of Blanchard posing that were being sent on to 'loads of women – and loads of women were sending images of themselves back, in poses of their own . . .'

Curious, Ahmed continued to search, uncovering more and more images of women posing for Blanchard.

So this was what the so-called family man got up to in his spare time! Ahmed, a devout Muslim, wasn't impressed.

Vanessa as a young girl.

Vanessa's parents, Sylvia and Roger. The couple met in 1969.

Presenting
The George Howard Sound
MUSIC TO SUIT ALL OCCASIONS

HOTELS, CLUBS, PRIVATE FUNCTIONS
ENGAGEMENT PARTIES AND
WEDDING RECEPTIONS.

All Enquiries to:-
George Farley—Organist/Pianist
24 Cecil Avenue, St. Judes, Plymouth PL4 8SG
Telephone: Plymouth 60345

Keep Music Live

An advertisement for the band with which Sylvia, Vanessa's mother, sang.

Singer's death at 36

THE former singer of one of the most popular bands in the Plymouth area has died after a long illness.

Sylvia Marks, who sang for 13 years with the George Howard Sound, died at St Luke's Hospice, Plymstock, on Sunday, at the age of 36. MAY 5TH 1985

Sylvia, who was noted for her unusual and adaptable voice, stopped singing a year ago when she developed a very bad cough.

She joined the George Howard Sound back in 1971 and quickly established herself as a very popular singer in a group which had great popularity, performing Saturday night spots at Plymouth's Holiday Inn every week during the winter months.

'Her death is certainly a bad loss to the George Howard Sound', said group leader George Farley, of Plympton. 'She is irreplaceable, largely because she had a most unusual voice which could blend to any type of song.

'Sylvia was very well respected by the band, and all the people that we sang for. She will be greatly missed.'

Sylvia, who lived in the Mutley area, of Plymouth, leaves a 15-year-old daughter.

The obituary which carried news of Vanessa's mother's death.

The house in Crozier Road, Plymouth, where Vanessa and her mother moved shortly after her parents split up. It was during this period that Vanessa encountered numerous babysitters while her mother was out singing at night.

Snapshots of Vanessa with her family at Christmas.

Vanessa poses with her mother and aunts.

Vanessa with her uncle, Barry.

Andrew George with his daughters, Pearl and Grace.

Just days after Vanessa's arrest, Andrew emerges from his Plymouth home a broken man after an alleged suicide attempt.

The house of horrors where Vanessa sent thousands of explicit emails, photographs and texts to paedophile Colin Blanchard from a cubbyhole just off the living-room area, as her children played and watched TV.

The social-networking site Facebook offered Vanessa an exciting and harmless escape from her work, but also introduced her to Allen and Blanchard.

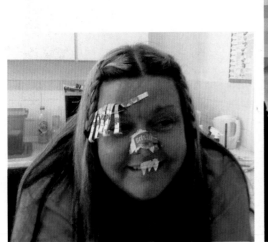

To her friends, Vanessa appeared to be a bubbly, fun-loving woman with a heart of gold.

Shamed. Vanessa attempts to shield her face as she arrives at court in a police van after her arrest.

Outside the court, public outrage and disgust bordered on violence, as furious parents and members of the community gathered to catch a glimpse of Vanessa.

Meanwhile, the media was in a state of frenzy.

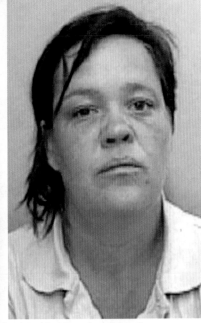

Vanessa George, Colin Blanchard and Angela Allen: three faces of despicable evil.

But then the nature of the images dramatically changed. Ahmed struggled to find the words to describe what he saw.

'When you first look at those things you just try and work out what it is. You can't work out what they are. Only when you saw a sequence and then it all unfolds what's been going on.'

Suddenly feeling sick, Ahmed immediately snapped the computer off as if even having the machine on could contaminate him with what he'd just seen. He still couldn't make sense of it, still told himself he must have been mistaken. Though he was surrounded by his work 'partners', he couldn't bring himself to say a word. He didn't want to tell them what he'd done, or, much more importantly, what he'd seen. For a few hours, he tried to put the images out of his head, as if by ignoring them he could make them go away, but later in the day he knew he had to look again, just to make sure of what he'd seen.

This time there could be no mistaking what was happening in the images contained in Blanchard's account.

Unsure what to do next, Ahmed asked around to find out where Blanchard was, only to discover his part-time 'partner' had gone to Dubai, without even letting him know.

Ahmed's feelings about the business betrayal were nothing compared to his angst over the images. Part of him still wanted to believe desperately that there was some explanation for them being there, that Blanchard hadn't known what they were, or hadn't been aware they were there. He knew that once he reported what he'd seen, there'd be massive consequences for the man he'd previously regarded as a business friend and for his family. Yet he also knew there was no choice.

With the heaviest of hearts, Ahmed picked up the phone and contacted Greater Manchester Police, who immediately requested that officers in Rochdale should prepare to raid Blanchard's home.

Greater Manchester Police took Noman Ahmed's call on 5 June very seriously indeed. Having ascertained that Blanchard would be travelling back from Dubai the following day, they lost no time in visiting the Trafford Park offices. Airport police were informed exactly when the businessman was due to be landing back from his Dubai trip and were waiting at Manchester Airport to arrest him.

The laptop and iPod he was carrying were both seized and, incredibly, both contained explicit images of very young, naked children, some being sexually abused. Colin Blanchard, it seemed, was so convinced of his own invincibility that he was flying around the globe with extreme images of child abuse, even to regions where those convicted of paedophilia might face the death penalty.

Detective Inspector Tony Creely, of Greater Manchester Police's sexual crime unit, explained: 'At the time of his arrest he had a laptop and Apple iPhone. These were examined by the high-tech crime unit. Examination of the items revealed a number of explicit stills of very young children. These images were of naked children of both sexes and believed to be at that time around twelve to eighteen months old, showing them being sexually abused.'

Blanchard was taken to a police station cell, where he would later be questioned.

On the following morning, Saturday, 6 June 2009, Blanchard's neighbours Richard and Susan Parker were on their way to church when they bumped into mousy-haired, bespectacled Anne Blanchard as she walked down a nearby street pushing her daughter in a pushchair. 'She seemed reasonably happy compared with the way she often was and it was nice to see her looking less stressed,' remembered Richard Parker.

Unknown to Anne Blanchard the police were lying in wait at the family home around the corner following their arrest of Blanchard at Manchester Airport as he'd got off that flight from the Middle East the previous day. When she returned to the house they swooped.

In the days that followed, neighbours and friends in the closely knit cul-de-sac where Blanchard lived were completely taken aback by the revelations that unravelled from the house. They were even surprised by the photo that Blanchard was using as his chilling calling card on Facebook. As Richard Parker said: 'The picture from Facebook was way out of date. He had aged a lot since then.'

No wonder Blanchard didn't want to meet his cyber-penpal Vee George in person.

Colin Blanchard was charged on Monday, 8 June 2009, with offences relating to the recovered images. Despite his cyber-protestations of love to her, Blanchard showed little loyalty, readily telling police that the images came from Vee

George, whom he'd met on Facebook and with whom he'd been trading abusive pictures.

With many of the pictures looking as if they had been taken recently, police realized the perpetrator of these images was probably currently active and they had to work quickly to identify them and halt any further abuse. They were also anxious to find this 'Vee George' before she got wind of Blanchard's arrest and destroyed any evidence there might be linking her to the photographs.

The problem was, they had nothing to go on. The photographs George had taken were all of children's torsos and almost impossible to identify. But careful scrutiny revealed one vital clue. Detectives noticed that in one photograph a tiny part of an emblem was visible on a shirt. Further research revealed the emblem was that of Little Ted's nursery in Plymouth.

Later, as police interrogated the hard drive of George's own computer, they would find the full logo on an entirely innocent photograph she had taken of a colleague at the nursery.

Noman Ahmed later revealed the full extent of his anguish over turning in his one-time friend Colin Blanchard. 'I was still giving Colin the benefit of the doubt. I said that if he was innocent and it was a mistake I would back him all the way.'

It had been left up to Ahmed to inform his business colleagues of what had happened and that was when the full nature of what Blanchard was accused of came home to Ahmed. There were half a dozen in the office and

Ahmed had the difficult task of explaining to them what Blanchard had done. They'd all had pending deals which required Blanchard's involvement.

One man was even going to be on the board of a charity helping abused kids. Ahmed described how 'He was gutted at the news. Through one deal with Colin he was going to put a percentage of the profits from their venture into that charity.'

Ahmed was left with no choice but to sell off stock and equipment and ended up giving a lot of it away because he didn't want any connection to things that Blanchard had touched. Blanchard had left some brand-new child safety seats which he had passed on to Ahmed. 'I just gave them to a charity. I didn't want anything to do with it. We cancelled contracts all round,' he explained. 'I just cut it all off because it wouldn't look good for them, because eventually Colin Blanchard would be mentioned. It would be bad for everybody if it all came out. I just wanted to make a fresh start.'

Ahmed admitted that reporting Blanchard had been 'probably the hardest thing I have ever done – but something I would have no problem in doing again'. Ahmed's own daughter had played a lot with Blanchard's daughter. 'Luckily my wife never lets my daughter out of her sight for even five minutes,' he added.

When Ahmed stumbled on the appalling child sex images back in June 2009, he also found it deeply upsetting because Blanchard had almost been like a family member. But these days Ahmed feels little emotion about the case: 'I feel proud that I have started something which has uncovered the truth for many and potentially saved a lot of young lives from abuse. These children are angels and by hurting them we hurt God.'

He continued: 'We had two businesses that we started, invested in, that I have now forgotten about and shut down. No money is worth carrying the guilt of knowing a person like this, whose actions would have only brought shame and disgust to my businesses and me. I have always believed that God will punish those who do wrong and as a Muslim I think Colin will get what he deserves for his actions.'

10

Shortly after 7 p.m. on 8 June 2009 the Plymouth duty inspector, Russ Sharpe, took a call which made him stop in horror. Just twenty minutes beforehand, the Devon and Cornwall police force's information room had been contacted by detectives from Greater Manchester Police. The call taker had jotted down the intelligence, creating a detailed log of startling information.

A reporter from the *Plymouth Herald*, Carl Eve, witnessed the George story unfold at first hand. Eve recalled: 'Control Inspector Russ Sharpe was on duty that night. He was the Papa One Zero control inspector for Plymouth but he was also the neighbourhood inspector for that patch of Laira as well. He had two hats on so he knew everything there is to know about the neighbourhood side and what happened that night. He's a very sharp Northern Irish guy.'

At precisely the same time, over at Plymouth's South and Central CID, detectives were working the late shift and dealing with a robbery case. Then they also took a glance at the updating log, with the same response as Inspector Sharpe.

In their call, Greater Manchester Police had intimated that Plymouth had a paedophile in its midst. The paedophile was female and she might well be working in the childcare industry and she was currently very active.

Inspector Sharpe remembered: 'As I read the log, my first impression was shock — and horror. We deal with lots of different incidents, but you rarely deal with one like this. I knew we were dealing with a critical incident.'

The nursery school — with nine staff and sixty-four pupils in total — was located within the grounds of a primary school, which had 284 pupils.

Eve later interviewed six police officers and was able to put together a dramatic timeline for the evening. These are his recollections: 'It was a bit like the TV show *24*. The report got typed up originally by Exeter call centre. Manchester phoned Exeter and they took about twenty minutes turning it around and typing it and then it was logged and the inspector in Plymouth was looking at it at the same time. They were getting on with their other job, which was a robbery. The inspector reads it from beginning to end and rushes upstairs and says, "Have you seen this?" and they all agreed there and then to take action that night.'

Carl Eve continued: 'Those officers had to ascertain where George was and her background and they didn't know if any of her colleagues were involved. They needed to get the nursery owner to secure the place with the keys and know where everything was such as light switches. They also needed to work out how they would interview her and make a proper plan of action.'

Inspector Sharpe immediately alerted Detective Sergeant Maggie Wood and her team, which included Detective Constable Sarah Lovatt and Detective Constable Nick Bloom. They quickly read the log as well and were already discussing what action to take. They all agreed that whatever they did, they must do it quickly. DS Wood remembered: 'I read the log and just thought, "Oh my goodness."' Then she called the detectives in Greater Manchester for more detail. 'We agreed, "We need to deal with this and we need to deal with it tonight, not tomorrow morning."'

By 8 p.m. Inspector Sharpe spoke to the out-of-hours social services worker in Plymouth. He related what officers had learned from Greater Manchester. A woman, from Efford, Plymouth, called Vanessa George, who worked at a nursery called Little Ted's in Laira, was connected with a man arrested for possessing indecent images of children.

George was suspected of not only abusing children, but also of photographing that abuse and forwarding it by both computer and phone. The social worker then began to study social services records in an attempt to track the nursery and its owner and establish where George actually lived.

Investigators feared that in just a few hours a new day would break and dozens of vulnerable children might be back under her care. Detectives also knew that Blanchard was to appear at court in the morning, which could further expose the situation to George. They feared that if she realized she would be next, she'd erase all her computer and mobile phone files, leaving little evidence for officers.

To make the arrest and be granted legal permission to search both the nursery and her home, police had to gather enough evidence to first approach a court clerk, before getting a warrant signed by a magistrate.

At the same time, other officers were working out the immense impact on the community. DC Bloom and DC

Lovatt continued making background inquiries, trying to identify George, her past record and any information about the nursery.

Inspector Sharpe explained: 'We knew we had to arrest her quickly. Normally you can take time to gather information, build up evidence to prepare for the arrest and interview. But we knew that in this case there was a risk the abuse could continue.' Sharpe asked himself: 'Would it have been right to allow her to go to work the next day and abuse more children?'

The social worker was shocked by the news when contacted by the police. He immediately spoke to his boss and they researched the nursery's background. As DS Wood described: 'It was a bit like journalists really. You get a name and you do everything you can to find out things about them.'

By 8.20 p.m., Superintendent Dave Sumner had been called in from his leave, as had Detective Inspector Costa Nassaris, head of the public protection team and an expert in behavioural forensic psychology. That summer DI Nassaris had been one of just twenty-four UK police officers to have gained the new postgraduate certificate in behavioural forensic psychology through the Child Exploitation and Online Protection (CEOP) academy.

The combined effort of Inspector Nassaris's expertise and Superintendent Sumner's authority to organize resources was crucial.

Officers were volunteering to stay on past their shift. Patrol officers stayed on. The office was full. Nobody wanted this one to slip through their fingers.

Meanwhile scene-of-crime officers were briefed. Then a media strategy was drawn up before research and paperwork was completed so officers were prepared for arrest and search. At around 10.30 p.m., an out-of-hours court clerk and a police officer travelled to a city magistrate's house and an arrest warrant was signed.

At precisely 11.11 p.m., around thirty officers gathered for a full briefing about the case. The arrest and search – which would eventually take all night and run into the next morning – was carefully mapped out. TAG and late-turn patrol officers were given the search tasks. The searches of George's home and of the nursery had to be carried out virtually simultaneously.

The investigation – codenamed Operation Morley – was to be led by one of the force's most senior investigating officers, Detective Superintendent Michele Slevin. She needed the evidence from the Manchester team to be in their possession to enable them to question George properly.

While the obvious method would be to send it via email, the team were conscious of both legal and security issues because sending the graphic images would mean they were technically committing the same crime – distribution of indecent images. Also, as no internet-based system is totally secure, the team could not afford even the slightest risk of the material going astray.

As a result, traffic officers from Plympton were asked to go on a blue-light run by special patrol car to Manchester to pick up the material on CD. Fortunately, Greater Manchester police assisted by bringing the evidence halfway, speeding up the entire process.

DS Wood explained: 'You only have a certain amount of time to interview people after arrest. You can't delay. You have to say what you have in interview, not what you think you have.'

Inspector Russ Sharpe then decided to take some well-earned rest, knowing full well that the next day would be a taxing one because he was the inspector for both the Efford and Laira districts of Plymouth, locations of the nursery and the George family home.

Sharpe would arrive back at 9 a.m. the following morning. A 'silver' meeting was arranged, to be attended by the Assistant Chief Constable and senior members of the local authority and the social and education services, which would discuss the impact of the case.

While officers set off to make the arrest, DI Nassaris and Superintendent Sumner drafted the letter, which would later be given to all parents whose children attended Little Ted's nursery the following morning, 9 June. It would explain the police action, promise to keep them all informed and give a contact number for the support being made available.

A detective from the Child Protection team – who has asked not to be identified – warned the detectives that the impact on the families would be very significant. He commented: 'We were also aware of her family, who had done nothing wrong.'

At 11.55 p.m. officers from the Child Protection team and CID hammered on the front door of George's home in Douglass Road, Efford. Stumbling out of bed, followed by her husband, she glanced out of the window on her way down the stairs. 'The police are here,' she commented flatly, before opening the door.

At the same time detectives had tracked down the owner of Little Ted's nursery, Angela Chudley, who was understandably horrified. One of them later told how 'We briefed her, but she didn't know the full extent of what had gone on. She then came with us with her keys to open up the nursery to our search team.'

Back at the George house, Andrew George was still half asleep and had no idea what was going on: 'My first thought was that someone had died. But there were so many of them. She [George] didn't look scared. She was cool, calm, focused.'

For some reason that Andrew George could not work out, the police wanted to talk to his wife. They took him out of the room while they sat her down on the sofa.

Then a police officer gently asked her: 'D'you know why we're here?' The nursery worker nodded with a calm, composed expression on her wide, jowly face. 'I don't want my husband to know,' she said, realizing even as the words came out that it was futile.

The police officers, keeping up the soft, considerate approach, then cautioned the woman sitting placidly on the sofa.

'I believe you've sent images,' the police officer began.

She replied: 'No, just photos of children.'

'You know I'm going to have to arrest you.'

George looked thoughtful. 'I got suckered in big time, didn't I? Is it Colin Blanchard?'

'Who is Colin Blanchard?'

'It doesn't matter.'

DC Lovatt said afterwards: 'She knew why we were there. She knew what we needed and what was going to happen. She made some significant disclosures to us. In fact she couldn't be more helpful to us at that time.'

At 12.05 a.m., Vanessa George was formally arrested on suspicion both of making and distributing indecent images of children and of sexual assault by penetration.

'It wasn't penetration,' she exclaimed suddenly.

Then, realizing that the house was going to be searched, she remarked: 'There's nothing in my house, my phone is in my pocket', before repeating: 'I've been suckered in big time.'

Andrew George was then brought back into the living room. Still clueless about what was going on, he gazed searchingly at his wife. It was then that she looked straight at her husband and calmly made the confession that would shatter her family's world for ever.

'Basically I got befriended by a bloke, who said I want you in my life and I took photos of children for him. I'm sorry.'

As Andrew struggled to take in what his expressionless wife had just said, she repeated once again: 'I'm sorry.'

Her voice was empty and emotionless.

'I don't understand,' he gasped.

Unfortunately, he would soon understand only too well what his wife was being accused of and why all these police officers were swarming over the house. While he was still trying to absorb what was happening, police continued talking gently to his wife.

'I knew this would happen,' she said abruptly. 'I can't believe what I've done.'

George told police that her family hadn't known anything about what was happening, before offering to hand over her Samsung, her so-called 'fun phone', informing them that it was a pay-as-you-go. She also told them about several email accounts she'd set up.

In between almost matter of factly providing information to police officers, George displayed sudden bursts of self-awareness:

'I'm disgusted with myself,' she burst out, and repeated: 'I can't believe what I've done.'

The task of the child protection officer, along with DC Lovatt, was to ensure they got as much information from George as possible during her interviews. Both said the initial approach was 'absolutely key' in building up the right atmosphere for obtaining information from any suspect.

DC Lovatt explained: 'Normally when a police officer comes to your door the response is "Who's died?" At least, it is if you haven't done anything wrong. She sat down and the child protection officer was gentle with her, asking you know why we're here, and she nodded.'

After a while, George was allowed to get changed and go to the toilet, although she was accompanied by a police officer.

All this time, her daughters, Pearl, fifteen, and Grace, thirteen, remained asleep upstairs, unaware that their lives were about to be turned upside down. But, with the police waiting to search the house, the moment when their innocence would be shattered for all time could no longer be put off.

A few moments later a still traumatized Andrew George knelt by his daughters' beds and shook them gently awake.

'Girls, girls, I'm going to take you up to Nan's house for a while.'

Sluggish with sleep, the two girls gazed uncomprehendingly at their father. They had to get up for school in a few hours, what on earth was he doing waking them up? They'd be shattered the next day.

Pearl and Grace exchanged confused and worried looks as their dad walked out of their room and downstairs, where they could now hear muffled voices.

It began to dawn on them that something was seriously wrong. Hearts pounding, they walked out onto the landing, where a woman they'd never seen before tried to engage them in conversation about school, as if it were the most normal thing in the world to be woken up in the middle of the night.

Stumbling downstairs, the girls were shocked to find five police officers sitting in their living room as well as their parents – their father pale and shell-shocked, their mum oddly expressionless.

A plain-clothed policeman in burgundy shirt and black jeans knelt in front of the frightened girls and told them everything would become clear in the morning. Perhaps guessing that this would turn out to be something they'd far rather not know, the girls didn't ask questions but mutely left the house accompanied by a policeman, their father and their pet dog Georgie, a two-year-old border collie. To their distress they weren't allowed to take anything with them, including their precious mobile phones.

Stepping into the cool night air, the girls gazed with alarm at the riot van parked outside their house, but they didn't have time to wonder about it as they were quickly ushered into the back of an unmarked police car and driven to Andrew's parents' house.

'What's going on?' Grace turned to Pearl, but the older girl had no answers for her sister.

Vanessa George's mother-in-law, Dorothy George, was deathly pale as she answered the door in her dressing gown. She hugged the girls wordlessly and led them into the living room while she and her son Andrew and husband Bill talked in the kitchen, their urgent whispers filling the listening girls with dread.

Andrew George decided to spend the night at his brother Philip's house nearby. His daughters clung together after he kissed them goodnight. Grace had tears streaking down her cheeks.

In the kitchen, their granny Dorothy was sitting with her head in her hands, still reeling from everything that had happened and dreading the conversation she knew was coming. Cuddling her granddaughters, she tried to put into words the unbelievable facts that Andrew had just given her.

'Your mum has been taking pictures of kids – indecent images of them.'

How could two young girls possibly comprehend the incomprehensible? That the mother who used to pick them up from school when they were little, and tuck them into bed at night, had been accused of taking indecent photos of the babies and toddlers in her care?

That night Pearl and Grace lay on quilts on the floor of their grandparents' house, grateful for the peace after the drama of the previous few hours and desperate for the blissful oblivion of sleep, hoping against hope that when they awoke the next morning it would all turn out to be a horrible dream.

Their mother had been taken to Charles Cross Police Station for further questioning by the child protection officer and DC Lovatt. The two interviewing officers had to devise a series of questions which would get George talking. They knew it was essential they extracted as much information as possible from her before she started to refuse to co-operate, as so often happened with suspects.

At first, they both found George to be 'calm, amenable, friendly . . . the way you would expect a normal member of the public to help the police,' DC Lovatt later recalled.

DI Nassaris said officers were well aware that this could have been a 'front to the world, to manipulate people'. They also knew it was not uncommon for suspects to admit to less serious offences to stop officers digging any further. Nassaris explained: 'When confronted by this situation, if she comes across as a helpful person, then she's trying to groom us, con us. Probably that's how she's groomed the people around her.'

George was remarkably quick to judge her own actions, describing them as 'vile'. 'I'm fuming with myself really. I am,' she said, as if she were chastizing herself for accidentally leaving the iron on while she went out, instead of deliberately targeting young children for sexual abuse. 'It's the epitome, isn't it? It's like, absolutely disgusting.'

While outwardly professional, the detectives were themselves struggling to come to terms with what was before their very eyes. Lovatt later said that 'We've all seen hundreds and hundreds of these awful photos, but it's very, very rare that you find the offenders who made them and is actually in the photo as well. To find them, and for it to be a woman, for her to be here in Plymouth, working in a nursery? It's incredible. But we're police officers – we have to treat them professionally, whatever the situation.'

The child protection officer, who had years of experience dealing with child sex abuse offenders, nevertheless admitted to being 'shocked and disgusted': 'In regards to some of her chat and email messages it was horrendous. If you looked at some of the things they were fantasizing about, they were very disturbing from our perspective. It's almost difficult for officers to get their head around her being able to do that in the position she was in.'

The initial interview with George concluded in the early hours of 9 June at Charles Cross Police Station and she was taken to the cells for the night.

But for the detectives on the investigation, sleep was in short supply. While the arrest had gone without hitch, they still had to tackle a full search of the nursery – and how to break the news to the parents.

DI Nassaris and Superintendent Sumner's carefully drafted letter had to be given to all parents who attended Little Ted's nursery later that morning. Meanwhile detectives were already with the nursery's owner, Angela Chudley, who opened up the premises for a police team.

While George had undoubtedly been helpful and

forthcoming when first arrested, by the time she was brought in for interview a second time later on 9 June she'd undergone a complete turnaround in attitude.

DC Lovatt remembered: 'One thing that struck me the most was the change in her. The first interview she was chatty, friendly, couldn't be more helpful. I was on cell watch and she was talking and chatting and laughing. The next day, the difference was incredible. Her personality had closed down. There was nothing there. It was like it was two different people. It was like she took one mask off and put another one on.'

George had retreated into a sullen and almost total silence.

11

At 6.05 p.m. on the same day as her arrest, 9 June 2009, George was interviewed by police but this time her solicitor was present and her entire demeanour was different from a few hours earlier.

The interview began with her being read her rights.

POLICE: Are you happy you've had enough time to speak to your solicitor?

VG: Yes.

POLICE: OK. And you're happy to go ahead with the interview?

VG: Yes.

POLICE: If I can just recap what was said last night, in relation to the comments that you've made. We've had to disclose that to your solicitor today, and talk in general. Do you want to just tell us again what you said last night?

VG: No comment.

The police then referred to comments which George had made in the previous interview in which she claimed she had been duped by Colin Blanchard into taking pictures of children in her care at the nursery. To a series of detailed questions, George repeatedly replied: 'No comment . . .'

POLICE: You're happy you've had enough time to speak to your solicitor and seek that advice?

VG: I have . . .

The police then talked to George about her internet history and she provided a password to an internet account.

POLICE: Can you just tell us who you've been chatting to online?

VG: No comment . . .

POLICE: You talked to us last night, what's changed?

VG: No comment . . .

POLICE: Do you want to add anything to the 'no comments' that you've made so far.

VG: No.

Interview ends.

Less than three hours later, at 9.22 p.m., officers tried again to get George to open up but she was now proving an even harder nut to crack. The interview began with her being read her rights once again. But this time her solicitor read a prepared statement on behalf of George, in her own words, in which she denied penetration of any children.

SOLICITOR: . . . It was love and affection that I felt for him [Colin Blanchard] and it was back from him. He said he wanted me in his life and when I asked if there could ever be a future for us, he said 'yes definitely' . . .

George herself then continued.

VG: He asked me for a picture of a child as he knew I worked at a nursery ... I sent him two or three ... I did this because I knew it would make him happy, I felt disgusted really, but did it anyway. The relationship between Colin and I became difficult, strained, because I couldn't trust him, so in order to keep him happy I just sent him more pictures.

. . .

POLICE: ... Parents have gathered this evening and the police have tried to speak to these parents and reassure them and there is a great deal of worry about. They want to know Vanessa if their child has been harmed, if you've taken a picture of their child and it would help them, and yourself I think, to get that burden off your shoulder further. Which children did you take pictures of?

VG: No comment.

. . .

POLICE: ... what I'm concerned is that not only have you worked as a nursery nurse, or a nursery assistant whatever it's called, but you've worked and you've baby-sat and cared for other children, either at their home or in your home and that's what I've asked you to try and expand on earlier on. Do you not care at all?

VG: No comment.

POLICE: You don't.

. . .

Detectives then showed George images of children being abused.

POLICE: Did you take this picture?

VG: No comment.

POLICE: Their mother has a right to know, their father has a right to know and you're not helping them.

. . .

POLICE: What was your thought process, did you think 'this is getting too weird now, this is all wrong, I've never done anything like this before, I've got two children of my own?' . . .

VG: No comment.

POLICE: Did you think 'I've just taken a photograph of a naked child, what on earth have I done?', did you have that thought process?

VG: No comment.

POLICE: Did you think 'Colin's going to love me a little bit more now, because I've taken a photograph of a child, if that's what he wants from me and that will make him love me a little bit more', is that what you thought?

VG: No comment.

. . .

POLICE: Why didn't you run a million miles in the other direction? . . .

Interview ends

The following morning, at 11.23 a.m., George was interviewed for a fourth time. This time she was read her rights by detectives and was told her mobile phone had been recovered and 'rushed' to the Forensic Telecommunications Service for analysis. Detectives began questioning her about indecent pictures of children.

POLICE: We've talked already about the pain that the children must have suffered . . . Vanessa? At the moment you're staring down at the floor, not answering anything I say.

SOLICITOR: I'm afraid I'm going to intervene just one moment because I don't wish this to become too oppressive, with pressurizing the client . . . we'll answer your questions, but I still don't think that was a question.

POLICE: OK . . . Did you realize you caused pain to those children?

VG: No comment.

POLICE: Did you do it for your own sexual pleasure?

VG: No comment.

Police then asked George why they had recovered images of abuse of children from her phone and when she took them. They also asked her when she started having 'sexual thoughts towards children'. Her solicitor again warned that the interview was becoming 'oppressive' and that police 'cannot plead with the subject for too long'.

POLICE: Having spoken to us in your first interview, you have declined to talk to us again, you've given us a prepared statement and gone 'no comment' throughout the rest of the time. You've not in any way assisted the police in identifying any of your victims, the most vulnerable members of society, who you had a duty of care over in that nursery. I asked you in the first interview about your training in relation to child protection and you said that you had some but you couldn't remember the full details. Do you accept that you had a duty of care to look after those children in the nursery?

VG: No comment.

POLICE: Parents were trusting you with the most precious thing they have, a child . . . Do you understand?

VG: No comment.

POLICE: . . . The children in your care could well have images circulating round the whole world now. You've already distributed those images to a man who has a sexual interest in children. I am just trying to understand why you did what you did, trying to work out what made you do it and the person behind it. Is there anything at all that you'd like to say to us?

VG: No comment.

. . .

POLICE: We're looking into offences of making indecent images, distribution of indecent images, sexual assault, sexual assault by penetration.

. . . Have you any information you can now furnish me with, which would ultimately assist the Crown Prosecution Service in making decisions not to prosecute in this matter? Do you want to add or clarify anything to what you've said so far?

VG: No comment.

When film tapes of all George's interviews were later released by police to the BBC's *Inside Out South West* programme, they caused an outcry because they seemed to reiterate just how cold-blooded this mother of two really was. And George's claim that her motive was that she hoped to one day marry Blanchard didn't cut much ice either. George suggested her continued complicity was partly to keep his attention. But she steadfastly refused to name or identify any of her victims.

POLICE: Help the families who are out there now. Stressed, worried . . .

[*Silence*]

POLICE: Please help us and tell us who you took pictures of.

[*Silence*]

POLICE: Vanessa, please. For them.

[*Silence*]

POLICE: As a mother you'd want to know. Don't you care?

VG: No comment.

POLICE: You clearly don't. I can't believe you can sit there and not care.

Interview ends.

Later, one of the two officers present during all the interviews with George said the thing that bothered him the most (and he had been doing child abuse cases for five years) wasn't the photos but the email conversations that basically talked about S&M on children. It was the graphic description of what they would do to children.

Over at her in-laws' home, the Georges' daughters had awoken that morning to the sickening realization that the events of the previous night had not been some sort of nightmare but were all too real. Andrew George was back to tell them their home was being searched, and would continue to be searched over the next couple of days. It felt like every part of their previously normal family life was being violated and tainted.

Later on that morning a social worker came with a policeman but to the girls' relief they weren't being taken into care. They were also allocated a police liaison officer, as the story was about to go public and there was huge concern about the effect it would have on the family.

The police liaison officer gently gave Andrew George a fuller account of what had happened. 'He said Vanessa had allegedly been taking pictures of children and sending them to other people,' Andrew George later recalled. 'I asked, "What, paedophiles?" and he said, "Yes." As soon as I used that word, I couldn't believe it.'

It was the word 'paedophile' with its powerful moral connotations that led Andrew to finally acknowledge what his wife had done. Then, naturally, came the next question: 'If she'd done that to other children, could she also have abused her own?'

Wretched and mortified, Andrew had to approach his still traumatized daughters and ask them: 'Do you remember anything, do you think she interfered with you?'

To his overwhelming relief, the answer was no.

Up in Manchester that same morning following George's arrest, Colin Blanchard was appearing, via video link from Strangeways Prison, at Trafford Magistrates' Court, charged in connection with the images found.

In Plymouth, officers were poring over George's computers and mobile phone records, as well as searching through the family house and Little Ted's nursery. Realizing the potential enormity of what they were discovering, police set up a major incident room. The investigation would eventually include 550 actions, and during it 350 exhibits were seized and 950 documents examined.

Detectives desperately hoped they would be able to reassure parents and staff at Little Ted's that George went no further than the written word despite 'playing out' extreme sexual fantasies in thousands of texts and emails exchanged between her and Colin Blanchard. But as they began uncovering the evidence, photos emerged which made it clear that children at Little Ted's had been abused. Officers close to the investigation were stunned and horrified by the pictures George had taken. Despite his own vast experience, Detective Inspector Nassaris later admitted: 'I've been really shocked by the betrayal of trust and the sheer number of people who've been terribly affected by her actions.'

Not surprisingly the media were quick in sniffing out that there was something major going on down in Plymouth.

The Vanessa George case was about to explode.

PART FOUR
Law and Order

'Heaven never defaults. The wicked are sure of
their wages, sooner or later.'

Edwin Hubbell Chapin

I 2

Every parent knows how difficult it can be getting kids to the nursery on time before racing off for work themselves. So when the first parents arrived at Little Ted's early in the morning on Tuesday, 9 June 2009, their hearts sank at the sight of the locked gates. But when the police officers stationed around the unit on Bramley Road, Laira, handed them the letter explaining that a 39-year-old employee of the nursery had been arrested on suspicion of 'distributing indecent images of young children', impatience soon turned to horror.

The letter handed to parents and signed by Superintendent Dave Sumner explained that the nursery would be closed for the day while police carried out further investigations and included a phone number for parents to ring if they had any queries. 'I appreciate that this information will be of serious concern to you and it will be an important part of our investigation to keep parents and carers updated,' it concluded.

Parents, still clutching the hands of their toddlers or gripping the handles of buggies, gazed at one another in mute shock.

One mum whose two children attended the Little Ted's unit said: 'I got here and most of the gates were shut and

I heard a woman had been arrested. It's quite disturbing and scary.'

Another mum of a three-year-old who attended the nursery said: 'I was given a letter and told the unit should reopen tomorrow but I'm having second thoughts.'

Other parents had no such dilemma. 'I can't believe this,' said one outraged mother. 'I am never ever bringing my son back – not in a million years.'

Their son had first been enrolled in September 2008 and continued sessions there until the nursery was shut down on 9 June. On that morning the father drove past the nursery in Bramley Road on his way to work when he spotted a police cordon. His initial thought was the corner shop had been robbed, but a text from his partner later proved otherwise.

She said: 'I got handed this piece of paper telling me that a person had been arrested for having indecent images. My first reaction? I just thought it was pretty disgusting. I knew the name pretty quickly. All the other parents there were passing it on.'

Another mother was distraught at how her three-year-old would react if she withdrew him from the unit. 'He was getting on really well and liked it. They are like second mothers because I am not there. I don't trust anything right now. This is disgusting.'

Parents of children at Laira Green primary school, which was next door to the nursery, were also left reeling from the news, particularly as the day progressed and crowds of press and television crews gathered outside the school gates. Many of the children had recently passed through Little Ted's and most still regarded the staff as friends.

Of course, it didn't take long for the name Vanessa George to emerge. Parents were thunderstruck as they realized what the woman they'd universally regarded as fun-loving, bubbly and completely trustworthy was supposed to have done. As rumours began to circulate freely, the anger and frustration soon grew.

'Why won't they tell us anything?' anxious parents asked one another. And underlying every conversation, there was always the same unspoken question: were any of their own children in those photographs?

'Part of me just wants to know if my little girl was one of the victims,' another mother told reporters. 'The other part keeps telling me I'm better off not knowing. It's the uncertainty that's tearing us apart.'

Inevitably, after the shock started to sink in came the recriminations. Should they have been more vigilant? Had there been warning signs?

Parents started to think back on times the nursery had appeared to be understaffed. According to one mother, there were too few adults supervising too many children and the result was often 'noise and chaos': 'It wasn't unusual to see kids running around half naked, probably after weeing in their pants, or taking their tops off when it got too hot. They would probably never notice if Vanessa George slipped away with one of the children for a few minutes.'

Another mother recalled how George would sometimes greet her at the gates with her son on one arm and a bag containing his soiled pants in the other: 'She would just say there had "been a little accident" and that she'd had to change him in the toilet. It makes me shudder now even to think of them being together like that.'

Some parents felt that the geography of the nursery, with its two separate units, one in Laira United Church and the other in Laira Green primary school, might have unintentionally helped George to carry out her abuse undetected.

One mother described how if a child was upset, screaming and crying – especially on arrival – it wasn't unusual for one of the nursery workers, including George, to take the child off on their own to calm them down, away from the other children: 'You got the sense that if a child needs space it gets it. But looking back, if you wanted to target a child, it'd be easy. Just pinch them, get them to cry and say, "Oh, I'll take them off."'

Suddenly parents were remembering the times their children had been reluctant to go to nursery. Was that because terrible things were happening to them there?

'Just before all this happened I dropped our son's hours,' recalled one father. 'He had been full-time for quite a long time but suddenly hated Mondays. About the week before I dropped him to half-days. It was just awful getting him to go. He'd been full-time for all of twelve months and suddenly he just hated it – hated Mondays.'

He went on: 'Your kid's crying and screaming at the front door. And the other children are getting upset and then someone takes them off to calm them somewhere quiet. You're grateful and so are the other staff, but looking back you think, "Was that when it happened?"'

'You trust them because they've been there for years. I know of one child who idolized Vanessa. If Vanessa wasn't there they would cry. Of course, you later question it all, all your child's behaviour. At first you just put it down to them being children, but now we don't.'

That Tuesday evening – less than twenty-four hours after George's arrest – there was a special closed meeting at St Paul's church, Efford, attended by scores of police officers and other community officials. More than a hundred anxious parents and relatives packed the church hall desperate to find out more about what was going on. A scrum of cameras and reporters were ordered to remain outside the building.

Some families were ready to go across the road and punch the photographers and cameramen if they didn't leave them alone. One police officer later said that 'We had to go over and tell the media to put their cameras down for a bit to calm things down.'

Another detective later recalled going into that first meeting at St Paul's church: 'It was very tense. There was a lot of grief and upset. But it wasn't directed at the panel. People wanted answers and guidance. Sadly, I think it's fair to say I don't think anybody got everything that they wanted from that meeting.'

Plymouth's District Commander, Chief Superintendent Jim Webster, spoke to parents and those associated with Little Ted's, along with Plymouth City Council's director of Services for Children and Young People, Bronwen Lacey. She praised the parents' 'measured' response to the 'shocking' news.

Meanwhile police spoke to staff at Little Ted's and other parents of children at the centre in the hope of piecing together more evidence of George's heinous crimes. Bronwen Lacey also told the meeting that a team of social workers, educational psychologists, health visitors and other health professionals was being brought in to liaise and work with the families. 'The local Safeguarding Children Board has activated a team of professionals and staff to co-ordinate our response to whatever the parents and children need,' she said.

Afterwards, she explained: 'We gave them information that was quite shocking. We were able to tell the parents there was no planned date to reopen [Little Ted's]. We need to discuss with Ofsted when the nursery can reopen . . . when and if it will reopen.'

Recalling that first meeting in St Paul's church on the night after George's arrest, Detective Inspector Costa Nassaris commented: 'One can only imagine how those mums and dads felt.'

Many parents demanded that police ask George directly to identify all the children she abused, to save the families from further worry and put them out of their misery.

DI Nassaris refused to reveal what had been said during the interviews with George, but many interpreted his apologetic demeanour as proof of the contempt the police felt towards George for saying nothing and extending the suffering for both parents and their children.

The meeting had been held to pre-empt some of those disturbing details. Chief Superintendent Webster explained: 'The parents heard shocking information. But to try and go into detail to over a hundred parents and relatives, and to manage the consequences of their reactions – it is new ground for all of us and indeed the whole country. Now we need to try and think about the needs of the particular families. We need to tread carefully as we go.'

Afterwards, he added: 'We took the opportunity to allay their fears where possible and also further the police investigation into the allegations. We will continue to liaise with local groups and people associated with the nursery and are committed with our partners to update concerned and interested parties at the earliest opportunity.'

Emotions were running high at the meeting, where police tried to allay fears wherever possible but admitted it was going to be a very long process with both units of the nursery remaining closed for the foreseeable future while they tried to speak to many of the parents individually, painstakingly making sure they contacted everyone who'd had a child registered there during the crucial period. During the meeting some parents left the church hall in tears and others had to be comforted by officers.

'But how will we know whether it's our children in those pictures?' was the question that kept being raised again and again.

There was no real answer that police could make apart from to give parents of children who had been most at risk – those under three who attended the nursery between certain dates – a list of 'criteria' of symptoms that victims of the abuse might show.

Although no children had yet been identified in the

images, a multi-agency support network was quickly set up in Plymouth to offer advice and guidance.

At the emotionally charged meeting was Kathy Hancock, chair of the Heart of Efford Community Partnership. Afterwards she spoke to reporters: 'The families have shown a high amount of dignity. It could have become riotous but they have been a credit to the community. This is every parent's nightmare. It's been really hard to see parents going through this.'

Hancock and Sue Haswell, a parent support adviser, had been drafted in by the police to help feed information to the community. They praised the police investigation and the sympathetic way they had dealt with parents and the community. 'At that first meeting there was a lot of disbelief,' Kathy Hancock later recalled.

Little Ted's nursery remained closed in the days following George's arrest. Devon and Cornwall Police issued a statement that officers were still continuing to speak to staff at the nursery and its future was left hanging in the balance.

While Plymouth was trying to get over its collective shock and rally round the children and families at the centre of the scandal, television crews from around the country and indeed the world continued to flock into the area, drawn by a story that threatened to challenge every stereotype both of paedophilia and of nurturing motherhood.

Many bewildered parents were doorstepped by journalists and conveyed their feelings for the world to hear. The day after George's dramatic midnight arrest, one couple who lived near Little Ted's told how they knew some of the nursery staff already, with one being a close friend, which had always made Little Ted's an even more ideal place to leave their children. They had already sent their middle child to the nursery and when their youngest came of age, they were equally content to choose Little Ted's.

Some parents admitted they wished George could be coerced, or even conned, into giving names. One father pleaded: 'Perhaps they could tell her she'd get time off if she named the children, so the parents could just be allowed to deal with it. I know one dad who said, "Oh, it's not our son, because he would say something", but you can't be sure.'

The same father added: 'Our son has never liked her anyway. He's got a couple of favourites and that's it. There's a few others he didn't like, but he certainly didn't like her. The police have been good about the whole case. Their reaction at the beginning, moving so fast, is commendable. We get texted up-to-date developments from the police. They're keeping us informed of things as best they can.'

The mother of the same child said: 'I just keep looking at my son and thinking, "How could you do it to him . . . it's sick." The irony is I've always been protective of my son – always. He's always in eyesight of me. If I can't see him then that's it, I'm in a panic.'

Many parents found themselves going over old ground, revisiting tearful goodbyes, the excuses to stay home. One mother said: 'Not long after he started going to nursery, our son started saying, "Don't want to go, I've got a bad back", and you later think, "What three-year-old says they've got a bad back to get out of nursery?"'

One couple explained their concerns about how – or if

– they should raise the matter with their son. The father said: 'We've thought about taking pictures of him to see how he reacts. Should we test it, ask him, "Did anyone do this [take pictures] of you at nursery?" We wondered would he recognize her, would he be able to remember anything? Or will he remember things later on?'

While some parents questioned the role of George's co-workers, others who knew a number of the staff personally made a point of praising them. One mother said: 'I don't blame any of the others. I put my child in a nursery to be looked after. I've got one very good friend who works there, I've known her for years, and my son would always be around her.'

The father recognized the staff's predicament: 'They may lose their jobs over this and it wasn't even their fault. But if rules were followed it wouldn't have happened, would it? Where I work, mobile phones are not allowed.'

The day after George's arrest, her family visited their Efford home with their faces covered to avoid the prying cameras of dozens of journalists, who'd been staking out the house ever since the news first leaked out. Andrew George and his two daughters were driven in an unmarked car by the police family liaison officer, Detective Constable Paul Dobinson.

DC Dobinson explained to the waiting press pack: 'Obviously, they are in pieces. It's been a massive shock to everybody, grandparents, the daughters and the husband. They are just taking it from day to day.'

It was unusual that a family liaison officer should be

allocated to a suspect's family, but under the circumstances it was felt that they needed support. As they dashed back out to the waiting police car, the two girls covered their heads with coats and blankets. Andrew George wore a parka with the hood up and a scarf across his face. He took time to lock the door but kept his head down.

Later that afternoon officers returned twice to the house, collecting bags of clothes and bedding, and later Andrew George's car. DC Dobinson told reporters: 'They will be staying at another address for a substantial amount of time.'

Vanessa George's blue Vauxhall Astra remained parked outside the house and had one window covered by tarpaulin. Broken glass was on the floor next to the missing passenger window, which had been smashed by police officers who wanted to search the car and couldn't find the keys.

At 12.43 p.m. on 10 June, George, still being held at Charles Cross Police Station, was charged with seven offences – two counts of sexual assault by penetration, two counts of sexual assault by touching, and three further counts of making, possessing and distributing indecent images of children. She was scheduled to appear the following day at Plymouth Magistrates' Court to hear the charges.

At a press conference later that afternoon, Devon and Cornwall Police publicly confirmed both that their investigation was focused on the exchange of material between George and Blanchard and that some of the indecent images which passed between the two had been taken inside Little Ted's nursery.

Chief Superintendent Jim Webster, from Devon and

Cornwall Police, told reporters: 'This investigation is fast-moving and now confirmation has been received of evidence leading to the charges today. It is a significant and disturbing situation and the position is made even more difficult that identification of the children in the images is very difficult. There are many that contain the images of torsos.'

Webster told the media the investigation had quickly determined links to George and it had been decided to take action immediately. He confirmed to reporters that the images were of 'young children, pornographic, illegal images and sufficiently concerning that we mounted the investigation overnight'.

He added: 'Of course it is a concern to all of us that [the arrested woman] worked in a nursery. Our work now is to find out what has happened, where the images have come from, where they have been sent to, and any risk to anybody in Plymouth.'

Chief Superintendent Webster stressed that the investigation was still at a 'very early stage' and refused to rule out making further arrests: 'The investigation will go wherever it needs to go. Our main priority is to stop the abuse of children, stop the taking of illegal images, and the route of the inquiry will go wherever it needs to go.'

By this time families of Little Ted's children had had more than twenty-four hours to process what had happened, and initial disbelief had built even further into frustration, anger and outrage. They'd thought they were sending their kids to a place where they'd be protected. They'd always assumed that whatever dangers were lurking lay outside the sheltered environment of the nursery.

So how had this been allowed to happen? How had a woman they'd all trusted implicitly and many had known socially been able to get away with abusing their children under the very noses of her colleagues and even take photos while she was doing it?

As the hours had gone by, and the shock subsided, the full implications of what had happened began to sink in. Those photos of their children were now 'out there' in circulation. Who knows who had access to them, or how widely they'd been distributed?

In addition they now had to think of how their children might be affected in the future if they turned out to be among the victims. It now appeared that George had targeted the youngest children as they'd obviously be unable to communicate what had happened. What were the chances they'd recover memories of the abuse at a later date? Did they subconsciously feel betrayed by their parents who, charged with protecting them, had unwittingly delivered them directly into the hands of a woman they now regarded as a monster?

13

By the morning of 11 June, with George due to appear in Plymouth Magistrates' Court, emotions amongst the parents were running sky high as they gathered outside the courthouse in St Andrew Street. Some had got there hours before the court was officially open, hoping to confront the disgraced nursery assistant, only to be taken by surprise when the white van in which George was travelling, complete with blacked-out windows, and a police car escort swung past them at 7.10 a.m., with George herself being bundled into the courtroom cells via a side entrance.

At around 8.40 a.m., ten police officers wearing protective helmets arrived at court in a van after a group of four to five youths began shouting outside the rear of the court. Police officers, wearing high-visibility jackets, spoke to the group, who left the scene and moved round to the front of the court.

Inside the courthouse, there was chaos as parents of the sixty children on the Little Ted's register jostled in the corridors with reporters and court officials. Three police officers stood guard at the entrance to the courtroom. The public gallery was restricted to thirty members of the public and, as people filed inside, full security searches were conducted by staff using a metal-detecting arch, wands and physical searches.

With space inside court number one restricted, two primary school teachers were allowed to feed back information to parents unable to get into the courtroom and court staff suggested that one person from each family went in to allow more families to be represented. One mother turned up at the court, but was unable to get inside: 'It really upset me that there were some people who went in who were completely unconnected with Little Ted's. I couldn't get in. It was only when the other parents came out and told us that we heard what she had done.'

At 10 a.m. George was brought up from the court cells wearing a pale cream, T-shirt-style top over black trousers, with her partially dyed blonde hair hanging lankly over her shoulders. She was flanked by two security guards and two police officers in the glass-shielded dock and kept her eyes firmly fixed on the floor.

The chair of the bench, Hilary Anderson, had already warned parents she would suffer no outbursts and would either eject them or clear the entire courtroom if there were any disturbances. 'This case is of a very sensitive nature and I would like to remind those in the public gallery that they should remain silent during proceedings,' she said. 'Anyone causing disruption will be removed from the court and if necessary the court would be cleared.'

However, for some parents, still battling to come to terms with conflicting emotions of shock, horror, guilt and gut-wrenching betrayal, it was all too much. Two rushed from the court in tears, even before the hearing began.

George spoke only to confirm her name, age and address before the charges were read out – two counts of sexual assault by penetration, two counts of sexual assault by touching, and one count each of making, possessing and distributing indecent images of children. All the charges were dated between January 2007 and June 2009, matching George's time at Little Ted's. One of the victims was a one-year-old girl. Another victim was an infant boy. Two infant girls were alleged to have been subjected to further assaults. Detectives from the investigation sat behind the solicitors listening to the charges being read.

As each charge was read out in full graphic detail there was increasing disquiet at the back of the court where those parents who'd managed to squeeze in were seated and were hearing the full allegations for the first time. One young father fled the court almost wailing in anguish, while others sat with their heads in their hands, their shoulders shaking with sobs.

Despite the warnings not to interrupt proceedings, emotions could not be suppressed. 'Monster,' one woman shouted. 'Sick,' screamed another. One man had to be restrained by police.

Throughout the ten-minute hearing George showed no reaction to the jeering and hissing from the parents sitting only feet away from her. Despite having been laughing and joking with many of them just days before, she never glanced in their direction, the only suggestion of any inner turmoil coming when she closed her eyes as the charges were being read out. She offered no pleas. Prosecuting, Michael French said George was of 'previous good character', while her solicitor, Geoff Parlby, offered no application for bail. At the end of the ten-minute hearing, she was remanded in custody to appear before Plymouth Crown Court on 21 September.

As George turned to be led down to the cells, for the first time she faced the public gallery. Parents erupted and began shouting at her, screaming her name and demanding that she look them in the face.

One man leapt from his seat and spat in her face as she was led in handcuffs to the cells.

Outside, the scenes got uglier as parents gave full vent to their pent-up fury. Several protesters broke through police cordons to bang on the prison van rushing George away. About forty people eventually chased the convoy down the road, hurling water bottles and shouting abuse. A police van in the convoy was flour-bombed.

Although police arrested two men – one in a suit, one in a red T-shirt – on suspicion of causing criminal damage and led them away in handcuffs, they were openly sympathetic to the parents' anguish.

The area commander, Superintendent Dave Sumner, said the vast majority had behaved with great dignity and restraint, despite suffering what he described as 'powerful and difficult emotions'.

Realizing how sensitive the situation was and how high feelings were running in the local community, police had deliberately adopted a non-confrontational approach. Officers on the ground were wearing police and public community bibs and local officers from Efford and Laira had been brought in to talk to the families to check they were well-informed.

A spokesman for Devon and Cornwall Police said: 'This is recognition that for many members of the public this is a distressing and emotional case, and there is a possibility that some people will want to vent their anger. The neighbourhood team is here to allow the public to talk to them so they can reassure them in a non-confrontational way. This is sensitive and we don't want to use a heavy-handed approach.'

After the van containing George had driven away, throngs of people hung around the court, crying and comforting each other. Some shouted abuse at waiting press and TV crews, but others simply sobbed and hugged each other.

Many were heard telling police that they had done a fantastic job, and how grateful they were for their efforts. Men, many in tears, embraced one another, while women clung together for support.

Following George's first dramatic court appearance, Chief Superintendent Webster openly acknowledged that many of the people who attended court had been left in shock as the details of the alleged offences were read out.

Police then revealed that experts who'd started examining the photos taken by George had confirmed that most of the victims were between twelve and eighteen months old. But, chillingly, detectives decided that because of the nature of the images they'd also ruled out showing the pictures to any parents who might have been able to recognize their children.

Tragically, the only recognizable 'symptoms' would be tell-tale changes in behaviour, which many parents now feared they had started to recognize in their own children. One mother, who believed her two toddlers were abused by George, said her children had become withdrawn but she only realized why when police told them about the allegations.

Officers gave all parents that list of 'criteria' mentioned at the meeting the previous evening, possible symptoms that victims of abuse might show, to identify those most at risk. That mother said: 'My children meet all those criteria. They have been showing symptoms of abuse. They are withdrawn, showing bad behaviour and wetting themselves. I am devastated.'

Kathy Hancock, chair of the Heart of Efford Community Partnership, had already met many of the parents at that first meeting after George's arrest. She had strong ties with the people in the troubled area, having lived and worked in Efford for more than twenty years, knew some of the families from the area personally and had known many of them when they were kids in Highfield school, where she herself had worked. She made a special effort to be present in the court when George made that first dramatic appearance. 'I remember one father at the court, he was so upset and angry. I just held him, because I remember him when he was a boy. There's a lot of families in disbelief and feeling guilty,' she said.

'Some have said to me, "Why did I let my child go to that nursery?" They are worrying about the times their child cried at the front door of the nursery. I mean, all parents go through that, don't they? But for these parents, because of this case and what they have heard they will torment themselves until this is concluded, until they know for sure.'

Kathy Hancock hailed the response by both Plymouth

City Council and the police as 'outstanding', recognizing that many support measures had been swiftly put in place. She herself had received dozens of phone calls from parents and grandparents.

'I think it was right for us to be there, to give them a bit of support because it was so tough. It's going to be a long hard summer for a lot of them. We had quite a lot come up to the church afterwards. They came to talk to each other, to console each other. They had to come to terms with what they had heard. One lady just ran outside and was sick. We had to try and reassure them, help them to carry on.'

Kathy Hancock was quick to state that Efford was already a strong community and, despite this trauma, would continue to stick together: 'We will all be there for each other. The investigation will continue and there will be a lot of families who will be involved and we will be there for them. I'm not just saying this because I live and work here, but you won't get a better community spirit anywhere – and that's what will get us through these difficult times.'

While the families of George's victims garnered whatever comfort they could from each other and from the support of their community, George's own family remained isolated, hiding from media scrutiny and afraid of reprisals. Following his wife's appearance at Plymouth Magistrates' Court, Andrew George released a statement through Devon and Cornwall Police in which he asked to be left in peace while he, his daughters and his parents and brother attempted to make sense of what had happened to them: 'Myself, my two children and family have been shocked by the information and events of the past three days. We remain strong as a family and will now await the case to go through the judicial system. We have two young children and my paramount concern is to lessen the impact these events have on them. We would ask that the media respect this and our privacy at this difficult time.'

But if Andrew George had been hoping that attention would shift away from his wife's crimes now that she'd been remanded into custody until September, giving himself and his daughters the summer in which to try to rebuild the shattered pieces of their lives, he was completely mistaken.

The Vanessa George circus was only just beginning.

14

Over in the Plymouth suburb of Plympton, Vanessa George's father, Roger Marks, was doorstepped by hordes of reporters who wanted to know all about the 'evil childcare assistant'. His initial reaction summed up how little contact he'd had with his daughter for the previous twenty years: 'This reporter came to the door and said something about Vanessa working in a nursery and I thought he meant she worked in a garden centre. I really didn't know what they were on about at first,' he said.

Meanwhile, in Douglass Road – where George and her husband had lived all that time – residents found themselves still being doorstepped by dozens of reporters. Some of George's neighbours were convinced revenge attackers might strike. One resident, Barbara Dean, said: 'I think there will be trouble once this gets around. They will petrol-bomb the house – that's what they're like around here.'

Her husband, Martyn Dean, told journalists that George's family were well-liked in the area, and used to go away most weekends to their caravan in Cornwall. But he then added: 'I dread to think what's going to happen now. This is a quiet little estate and I dread to think what kind of people might come round. I don't want any riots in my neighbourhood.'

Other neighbours described George as 'always very polite'. One went on: 'I always said she brought up her girls very well.' However, other residents of the street, which bordered a green space with a children's play park, remained concerned about the possibility of vigilante violence.

The city's police chief, Jim Webster, insisted to local residents that his officers were 'monitoring concerns in the community and we are making sure we have planning put in place for a whole range of eventualities'. Marked patrol cars were regularly driving past the George house in the days and weeks following George's arrest.

Plymouth child protection chiefs launched their own major investigation into the city's childcare provision following George's appearance in court. The Plymouth Safeguarding Children Board met after the shocking allegations were made public through the news media.

Members of the board, which included Plymouth City Council, Devon and Cornwall Police, Devon and Cornwall Probation, NHS Plymouth and the NSPCC, took part in an 'extraordinary meeting' to discuss the issues surrounding the investigation into the nursery worker.

The board pledged to carry out a Serious Case Review – normally only carried out following the death of a child. The board admitted the case was 'unprecedented' in their experience. The review was to run alongside the police investigation and was expected to take until the beginning of 2010.

At a press conference following the board's meeting, Bronwen Lacey, director of Services for Children and Young People at Plymouth City Council, said: 'This is unique territory. Universally, we are extraordinarily shocked at what we had to share with parents at the beginning of the week.'

The report would then be compiled from the review and an 'executive summary' made available to the public online. Lacey affirmed: 'We are committed to keeping children safe and we are very concerned that the charges laid in this case might indicate that the standards of safety we require have been gravely compromised.'

A helpline set up to assist both the police investigation and the concerns of families involved had already received more than 200 calls. Specialist services had also been put on standby for families who were in need of counselling and support.

Bronwen Lacey said nursery staff were also being supported: 'We are mindful too that we will have to care for the welfare of staff involved in the investigation as well as the children and their families. We need to hold on to the fact that the vast majority of children are very safe and happy and supported by staff who are committed to their health and well-being.'

George's innocent daughters, Pearl, fifteen, and Grace, thirteen, faced a difficult time back in the community following their mother's high-profile arrest. The girls had been taken out of their school after a few days because they were 'subject to the attentions of classmates', said one source close to the family. 'They had a very rough ride. The other kids were abusive to them and tormented them. They are innocent pawns in this whole sorry mess.'

One neighbour in Douglass Road told journalists her

daughter had been a good friend of the elder George girl: 'My daughter called round for her on Tuesday morning and a policeman opened the door. She did get a bit of a hard time at school for being friends with her. Children can be cruel like that.'

On 11 June the MP for Plymouth Sutton, Linda Gilroy, had a question on the Vanessa George case blocked by the Speaker of the House of Commons, Michael Martin. Gilroy was seeking an answer to a question relating to the case. Martin cut short the question and prevented the Leader of the Commons, Harriet Harman, from answering her.

Linda Gilroy was speaking about the reaction in her constituency after the police raid on Little Ted's nursery. During exchanges on future Commons business, she said: 'I am sure you will understand the shock, anger and disbelief of parents and indeed the whole community of Plymouth at the arrest earlier this week of a nursery worker and the charges today. The police and social services are clearly coming alongside to offer support but will you advise me and keep me informed of any appropriate opportunities to raise the issues which will inevitably flow from the concerns of the parents and the community –'

But the Speaker then intervened: 'Order! You may not know, or realize it, but this matter is now *sub judice* because there has been a charge and it is best that we move on.' Martin was referring to the court status of the case now that George and Blanchard had been charged and strictly speaking he was correct, but others saw his intervention as insensitive. It certainly proved that the whole country was reeling from the news of George's arrest.

On Friday, 12 June, Plymouth City Council wrote to parents across the city about the investigation into the Little Ted's case. The letter, signed by Colin Moore – assistant director of Services for Children and Young People – was sent to all the city's schools, which had been advised to distribute the letter to all parents and staff.

The letter gave details of how any families worried about the alleged paedophile activity could get support and explained that Little Ted's day care unit, where George worked, was a privately run nursery, and that the council only learned of the allegations against her following her arrest. '[The nursery] is not connected to the council and is not part of the nearby primary school,' the letter stated. It also pointed out that no other members of staff from Little Ted's were being investigated by police.

Meanwhile, families of children at Little Ted's continued to be spoken to by social workers and police family liaison officers. The Plymouth Safeguarding Children Board had already activated a multi-disciplinary team of professionals to co-ordinate the council's response to 'whatever the children, their parents and carers need'.

On Sunday, 14 June, photos of Vanessa George smiling and joking while wearing cut-up pieces of newspaper stuck to her eyebrows, nose and mouth hit the UK national newspapers. They showed a jovial, large lady with a pleasant expression on her face. Another shot showed George using the red rind of a cheese snack as a pair of pretend lips.

As one parent commented after seeing the photos: 'They say pictures don't lie. Well these ones do.'

Also on the first Sunday after George's arrest, prayers were said at St Paul's church, in Efford. The Reverend Steve Payne said the Bishop of Exeter had visited the church and a moment of silence was held at the beginning of the service: 'We had to remember the families affected by the events in Efford and Laira,' said the Reverend Payne.

When George's uncle, Barry Medway, heard about his niece's arrest he and his son – her cousin Lee – were both stunned: 'I talked to my son about what had happened to Vanessa. We always thought she was a bit neglected as a child but we never imagined that she would end up doing all these dreadful things.'

As a direct result of the Vanessa George case, the campaign for new cameraphone legislation throughout Britain's nurseries began to gain enormous momentum. Even in the few short days since George's arrest, a local mother and campaigner, Cheryl Higgs, had already succeeded in signing up twenty-three nurseries around Plymouth and Cornwall. As she said: 'There's a lot of legislation about cameras in pre-schools, but nothing about allowing or not allowing workers to carry their cameraphones in. I want to close the loopholes in the law.'

The debate over cameraphones in nurseries had been raging within the childcare industry for many years but it seemed that the George case had brought it all to a head. In an interview in a national childcare publication, Sue Meekings, director of childcare at Kiddi Caru, said staff in her nurseries 'know that having their personal mobile telephones with them in the playroom is potentially a disciplinary offence. When people are working they should not be sending text messages but it is also about not using them to take photographs. We are very rigorous that we only use the nursery's cameras and staff do not bring in their own cameras.'

Purnima Tanuku, chief executive of the National Day Nurseries Association, was reported as saying it was important nurseries had 'a clear policy for staff, such as if mobile telephones are allowed into the nursery and times they can be used'.

Little Ted's families continued to get regular updates and support from social services and the police. The distressing case had also brought many of the families involved closer together. As Cheryl Higgs later explained: 'Everyone knows everyone else now. Everyone knows each other involved, and we say hello and talk. It's really nice. People who you'd normally see at the school gates, you wouldn't have considered talking to them in the past, but now we're all talking to each other, waving as you see them in the street. It's very comforting.'

George had not been given bail, partly for her own safety, such was the public fury over the case among parents and relatives in Plymouth. Many of those who had attended George's remand hearing were still in a state of complete shock after the initial courtroom revelations and there was a genuine fear that someone might try to 'get at' George while she was in prison awaiting trial.

Immediately after being remanded to prison following

her court appearance, she was given special protection against attacks from other inmates, and in a bid to shield her from reprisals law officials deliberately sent her to the Eastwood Park prison in Gloucestershire, 150 miles from Plymouth. She was placed in a segregated wing and warned that she might be kept in it at least until after her trial later in the year. One source explained at the time: 'The case has received a lot of publicity and her face is now known. It is in everyone's interests to make sure she is protected so that she gets a fair trial.'

Back in Plymouth, the city remained in shock because of the case. Detectives were working around the clock to establish whether George had abused any other children before she joined Little Ted's. Police believed they had until her next court appearance in September to come up with new evidence.

Forensic investigators continued to hope they could identify some of the alleged victims from the photographs, despite the fact they showed no faces. 'They are looking for any clue that might help us identify them but it's going to be very difficult,' said one officer.

George steadfastly refused to co-operate with detectives in their quest to identify her victims. It seemed that she believed that if they could not identify the victims then she might be able to avoid some sense of responsibility for her actions. But as one detective pointed out: 'Nothing could be further from the truth. The longer George refuses to help us the harder it's going to be for her and the longer her eventual sentence will be.'

At Plymouth police headquarters, Carl Eve, the crime

reporter from the *Plymouth Herald*, was given further exclusive access to the Vanessa George inquiry team and spoke to Detective Superintendent Michele Slevin, just one week into the George case. Slevin had been in charge of an earlier and highly shocking case in Plymouth, that of the notorious millionaire paedophile William Goad (see page 302), and now headed the Vanessa George investigation, which had already attracted as much national attention as the entire Goad case had over a period of years.

Carl Eve vividly recalled what it was like in the Major Incident Room: 'The calmness belied the effort and complexity of the work being carried out on the investigation. Officers were only too keenly aware that just a few miles from their office there were around sixty families each of whom was riding an emotional rollercoaster of anxiety, anger, heartbreak, fear and sadness.'

Detective Superintendent Slevin stressed to Carl Eve that it was a 'fast-moving' case with many fresh developments. Even while they were talking, three more people were being investigated by Nottinghamshire police in connection with the investigation into Colin Blanchard and Vanessa George.

Slevin's team in Plymouth numbered sixteen, but that didn't include the neighbourhood officers or social workers from Plymouth City Council. She explained to Eve: 'We have child abuse investigators from Plymouth police as well as child protection and child services staff from the city council. The neighbourhood officers are integral to the investigation for the support they give to the families and the knowledge they have of the community. A lot of our information is coming from the families through their own neighbourhood beat teams.'

Those neighbourhood officers, led by Inspector Russ Sharpe, were the first on the ground to learn of unfounded rumours which could awake further anxiety in the community and set off the very revenge attacks that police so feared. Michele Slevin continued: 'Russ and his whole team are the face of the investigation, while the plain-clothed officers are working continuously in the background. We're using forensic service providers around information technology to interrogate telephones and computers.'

There were also officers from the Major Crime Investigation Team (MCIT). Slevin went on: 'Because of the complexity of the case and its high profile it was designated as a critical incident, which requires appropriate resources to be in place as well as experts and other agencies necessary to gather all the evidence available.'

MCITs regularly dealt with crimes such as murder or large-scale drug dealing, but Slevin told Carl Eve the number of families involved in the Vanessa George inquiry placed it in this category.

At the same time, Slevin said she was in communication with the individual senior investigating officers in Greater Manchester Police and now Nottinghamshire Police over all the latest developments in what was fast turning into a nationwide inquiry.

Despite recent reports in the press that Colin Blanchard would appear at Plymouth Crown Court alongside George in September, Detective Superintendent Slevin insisted at that time that there was 'currently no lead police force' on the three investigations, although she admitted one of her priorities was to probe any links between the other suspects and George in Plymouth.

At the meeting in St Paul's church only hours after George's arrest, she had promised the families she would try to keep them updated as soon as possible. She didn't want them finding out key developments via the media. Afterwards she admitted: 'But as this most recent development shows, it can sometimes be so fast moving that that's not possible in time. But we will continue to try and keep them updated, via text, personal visits, mobile phone calls.'

Slevin was keen to point out that affected families would continue to need support. 'They've been traumatized too and we recognize the distress and difficulties they have, from not knowing the full details.'

This was why police had set up the helpline, which fed into a multitude of partner agencies who'd joined together to support the parents, siblings, grandparents and extended families of those involved. Slevin added: 'We've spoken to them [parents] with other agencies who are providing support. We've told them there will be information we're not able to disclose because of the nature of the investigation, but that it's always for a very good reason. We have to recognize that information will get into the public arena which in turn may prejudice any potential trial and that's something we don't want to fall foul of.'

Slevin confirmed to the local reporter Carl Eve that all parents who could potentially have been affected had now been contacted. They had been visited by police officers and social workers to highlight the range of resources available to them, from alternative childcare provision to family and individual counselling. Police staff based in the call room, just yards from the Major Incident Room, meant investigators were kept constantly aware of what resources were being used by the families.

Detective Superintendent Slevin added that every snippet of information was added to the ever-growing mountain of data that officers were sifting through: 'We have to go through every bit of information in the room and it will continue to come in as we investigate. Inspector Sharpe and his team, along with our partners and my team behind the scenes, are working absolutely flat out to ensure all the evidence is gathered so we can bring about a successful conclusion. I know some of the families just want peace of mind and it will take time to do that.'

Any confusion about what George had actually done to those toddlers at Little Ted's had been cleared up in the most distressing way by the details that were revealed during her first court appearance. One mother and her husband had initially thought the case was about 'just pictures, just naked bodies'. She added: 'But then when it came out what was used on them, well it all took a turn for the worse. That's when I first started thinking, "Was it my child?" You would deal with it better if it was just pictures, but not other things.'

The father confessed: 'I've had a drink every night since this. I haven't stopped. I've gone through more bottles of vodka than before all this. I've tried to blank it out sometimes, but sometimes you just can't.'

He took time off work so that he could be with his son after the arrests and closure of the nursery. 'I'm pleased I had the time with him after it happened. Just being there with him, not to question him. But you do find yourself looking at them going, "What if you did get abused?"'

Both parents felt extreme anger towards George: 'People just want to kill her,' said the father. 'A lot of the feeling is because parents want to know, "What pictures and what kids . . . is it my child in that picture?"'

The mother revealed that, early on in the investigation, police asked parents if they could note down their children's 'distinctive birth marks'. 'But they haven't asked for anything else since. She [George] could at least have the decency to tell everyone whose child it was she abused and photographed, to stop all the worry. This could have gone on for ages if she hadn't been caught. You wonder if she's always been like this or did he [Blanchard] give her money to do this kind of thing?'

There were still *so* many unanswered questions.

15

Angela Allen is said to have gone 'white as a sheet' when her Facebook friends Colin Blanchard and Vanessa George were arrested on child abuse charges. A neighbour revealed that the Nottingham woman looked stunned when she heard on the TV news that police had raided a paedophile ring centred around a nursery school in Plymouth.

Greater Manchester Police officers had originally found the name 'Ang Bank' on Colin Blanchard's computer alongside some images of children being sexually abused. It took a week for officers to find out that this was Angela Allen, who had adopted the pseudonym because at one time she worked in a bank.

Just before midnight on 16 June Detective Superintendent Adrian Pearson, head of Nottingham Police Public Protection Unit, received a phone call at home, asking him to go to the home of Allen, who had been linked to a woman from Plymouth and a man from Rochdale who'd been accused of child exploitation.

'I was told that officers had identified links between Vanessa George, Colin Blanchard and Angela Allen and that a child was in immediate danger,' Detective Superintendent Pearson later recalled. Allen was mother to two girls, aged two and four. Police who raided Angela Allen's home found her and two men and they were all arrested on suspicion of making and distributing indecent images of children in connection with the Little Ted's nursery child porn and abuse investigation.

Detectives from Plymouth were being kept fully informed of developments by Nottinghamshire Police as they interviewed Allen and investigated the two men. Initially, police refused to reveal Allen's full address to the media amid fears that people still living there could be targeted by vigilantes. But officers quickly declared that none of those arrested had any professional contact with children.

Detective Superintendent Pearson said the two men who were arrested and interviewed had simply been 'in the wrong place at the wrong time' and they were released without charge.

Allen's neighbours had earlier watched in horror as officers took a computer out of her terraced home, as well as brown sacks and cuttings of carpet. A woman who lived nearby later told reporters: 'Everyone on the street is shocked. Nobody could believe it. You don't expect it. Police were all over the place. I have seen the woman quite a few times. She kept herself to herself. This is a family area. There are kids all over the place.'

But it quickly became apparent that the arrest of Angela Allen would be crucial in piecing together not just her own crimes, but those committed by George and Blanchard, hundreds of miles away in Devon and in Greater Manchester. Angela Allen admitted to detectives that she had met Colin Blanchard on Facebook nine months earlier and that he had introduced her to George three months after that.

As police swept through Allen's home they were surprised to find she had made no attempt to destroy the evidence, though she knew George and Blanchard had been arrested. She too, it emerged, was not just a consumer of the abusive pictures but had abused a child herself, recorded it and shared it.

After Allen's computer and phones were recovered, they were analysed as she was being interviewed about her relationship with Colin Blanchard and George. Allen was then charged with offences relating to sexual assault of a child and possessing child pornography. According to police, Allen had sent her two new friends – 'as a trophy' – an image which showed her raping a young child.

Back in Manchester, further examination of Colin Blanchard's computer revealed images of Blanchard abusing a child. He was re-arrested and charged with additional offences of sexual abuse. One police investigator explained: 'He intimated the pictures were intended for Vanessa George, and the pictures were found on the computer owned by Vanessa George too.'

In Devon, the senior investigating officer, Detective Superintendent Michele Slevin, told the media: 'We have carried out a large number of inquiries since our initial arrest on Tuesday, 9 June. This has resulted in the arrests in Nottinghamshire. From our current inquiries, there is nothing to suggest the most recently arrested people have any links to Plymouth or any premises in the city.

'However, we are still working to establish the exact links

that exist between these people and Vanessa George and evidence of the nature of their relationship. We are continuing to prioritize our inquiries here and we will now be working closely with our colleagues in both Greater Manchester and Nottinghamshire in relation to these arrests.'

Blanchard – who had earlier appeared before Manchester magistrates on child porn charges a few hours after George's arrest in Plymouth – was now officially set to appear alongside George at Plymouth Crown Court in September for a joint hearing.

On Saturday, 20 June 2009, Angela Allen appeared at Nottingham Magistrates' Court accused in connection with child sex offences. Dressed in a pink polo shirt, jeans and flip-flops, Allen appeared charged with four counts of sexually assaulting a child, four of taking indecent photographs, four of possessing indecent photographs, and four counts of distributing them. All the charges related to offences allegedly committed between April 2006 and 17 June 2009.

Clutching a tissue and a cup of water, Allen spoke only to give magistrates her address and date of birth during the five-minute hearing. She did not apply for bail and was remanded in custody until 6 July, when she would reappear at Nottingham Crown Court via video link.

Investigators had only just confirmed through examination of Allen's computer for the first time that her arrest was linked directly with the George case, in Plymouth, although no one would officially confirm any connection.

Back outside Allen's home in Nottingham, two policemen stood guard in case of trouble.

A few hours after Allen's court appearance – at just before 4 p.m. on 20 June 2009 – the Georges' family home in Douglass Road, Efford, was attacked by vandals. A small kitchen window at the rear of the property was damaged. Next day, national newspapers blasted headlines across entire pages claiming the house had been 'ransacked' but a local police spokesman later insisted: 'No entry was gained, the house was not ransacked as reported and we believe the culprits to be local children. The residents of Efford have been absolutely fantastic as far as we're concerned. They've remained composed throughout this very testing time for them all. We've had no reports of serious tension in the area and this is the first such reported damage to the property since the suspect's arrest.'

Police said the window, on the ground floor at the rear of the house, was boarded up, as was a front window as a precautionary measure. Devon and Cornwall Police's Chief Constable, Stephen Otter, praised his officers and the local community for their response to the arrest of George. Speaking at a police authority meeting, Otter said: 'The work that officers and staff have done in the community has been extraordinarily successful and I want to commend them for that. It is a very difficult situation. The police operation was carried out extremely well. The sense of grief and upset in the community will continue for a very long time.'

*

As worldwide interest in Plymouth and the Vanessa George case grew, parents of children from Little Ted's nursery found themselves suffering more and more anguish through George's refusal to name her victims. Every time another piece appeared in the newspapers or on the TV it reminded them of what might or might not have happened to their loved one. Some parents begged George to identify her victims. One mother told reporters that George should put parents 'out of our misery . . . She should give the names of her victims so myself and other parents can put this behind us and try to move on. It's not knowing that hurts the most. I pass Little Ted's every day to take my daughter to school and it makes me sick to my stomach. I hope to God my daughter wasn't one of her victims. My heart goes out to the other parents going through this nightmare.'

Another mother summed up the continual anguish that was haunting the families of children from Little Ted's: 'This disgusting woman has cast a shadow over us and that shadow will never be lifted. But it is made even worse by the fact that we don't even know who and how many children she abused. We have to know, otherwise our children will grow up and we and they will never be sure what happened to them.'

But George remained tight-lipped. Many of her own family and friends believed it was typical of the way she had run her entire life to date. One family member said: 'Vanessa would never face up to things. She'd rather put on a brave, jolly face, ignore the pleas and shrink back into her own twisted little world. I don't think she even appreciates the pain and anguish she is causing.'

Within a few weeks of the George case exploding into the public domain, police had contacted a social networking website company after members created 'anti' and 'pro' Vanessa George groups. The American-based website, which allowed friends and others to communicate and share information, was already hosting more than thirty groups relating to the nursery worker.

The majority of sites were overwhelmingly against the 39-year-old mother of two and one such group had already garnered more than 27,000 members. Another site claimed to know the contents of the pictures analysed so far. However, police insisted these descriptions were false.

The senior investigating officer, Detective Superintendent Michele Slevin, said officers were monitoring the social networking sites and recognized they could cause those families currently involved great distress: 'All details on the sites are being captured for review and contact has been made with the website hosts regarding removal of illegal or inappropriate material.'

In Plymouth, George's innocent fellow workers at Little Ted's continued to suffer from the fallout of her arrest. As Inspector Russ Sharpe later recalled: 'Some of the staff were governors of other schools, or took children on school trips. People have been saying they can't do that any more. They feel that they've been discriminated against. This case has had an awful ripple effect. The staff have been left in a very difficult position. Some have been hit three times: some had their kids there as well; they've been accused that as staff why didn't they know; and they've lost their jobs.'

Inspector Sharpe had even helped arrange a meeting for the staff and got some legal advice for them. Some could not get work now because other nurseries would rather not employ them. Some might never be able to work in the childcare sector again because of what had happened. Sharpe added: 'Fortunately, the staff know the majority of parents were very supportive of them. We asked if any of them had been abused in the street or whatever, but it's not happened.'

The main concern was that 'ripple effect' – people might take it out on the families or the kids of Little Ted's workers. Most of the children of staff or their siblings went to nearby Lipson school, so part of the police work as neighbourhood officers was to monitor community tension.

As Inspector Russ Sharpe pointed out: 'Managing community tension has been about listening. We had very, very little coming back to us that there were any problems. The neighbours up there [Douglass Road] have been good. To be honest we've had more reports of problems about press intrusion, causing more community tension than anyone else.'

Another tactic used by Inspector Sharpe was to ensure that neighbourhood officers from both patches – close to the nursery and the George family home – attended the magistrates' court when George appeared. The officers, who knew many of the families, had been there not for enforcement, but for support and even solidarity.

Inspector Sharpe added: 'It's also to reassure people that we were doing everything possible, because people's minds can change quickly. I think it was very good to hold the regular meetings, giving the parents the information.'

But the police knew the investigation was still a very long way from being complete. One detective openly admitted: 'There are still so many unknowns. We still don't have all the answers that we want and the parents want.'

Towards the end of June, national newspapers, including the *Sun* and the *Daily Mirror*, reported that an unidentified adult hand appeared in one of the pictures exchanged by George and her co-abusers Colin Blanchard and Angela Allen. One paper claimed that forensic experts 'would digitally enhance the poor-quality image to look for moles, birthmarks or scars that might pinpoint who it is'. And the *Daily Mirror* reported that one of the pictures taken by Blanchard showed two left hands, one of which remained unidentified.

But a spokesman from Devon and Cornwall Police later insisted that the image was not related to George or the Little Ted's nursery in any way. The spokesman said: 'We are satisfied that this image was not taken by George and is not connected to the nursery in any way. It's just a random image.'

Then on 2 July a 35-year-old woman from Liverpool was arrested by Merseyside Police allegedly in connection with the Little Ted's case. She was charged with indecent assault of a child under the age of thirteen and with making and distributing indecent images. But less then three weeks later – on 22 July – the case against her was dropped because of what the force described as 'insufficient evidence'. Shortly after the woman's release, police denied reports that another suspected fourth member of George's evil paedophile gang was still being hunted.

During the summer of 2009 a series of meetings were held with the families and the police, local authority and other agencies, to keep the Little Ted's parents informed of developments. In addition, Plymouth's investigative team set up an 'ethics' committee to look at what police should do to identify the victims from the images and what would be the most ethical way to achieve that.

The dilemma was two-fold: the police were understandably determined to solve the mystery of who had actually been abused; but, as one senior officer admitted, the methods police could use to identify children who were, in many cases, too young to understand or even appreciate what had been done to them by Vanessa George might be traumatic for them, especially if it turned out they had not even been abused.

'It was a no-win situation,' explained one detective involved in the investigation. 'Whatever approach we took was going to end up causing major problems, but as professional investigators we felt obliged to continue to press for the names of George's victims.'

It was clearly turning into the most difficult investigation any of the police would probably ever find themselves involved in. There were no precedents for the case and that meant investigators would have to tread very gently.

Up in Rochdale, the bank which lent Colin Blanchard a 90 per cent mortgage on his house foreclosed and put a fourteen-day notice period on his main car – a Range Rover

– as well as the property itself. Shortly afterwards members of Anne Blanchard's family arrived in a small furniture van and removed everything of value.

But nothing could prevent that house from representing the most horrible catalogue of child abuse.

16

Parents of children at Little Ted's found themselves in what must have felt like a never-ending emotional melt-down in the days and weeks following George's arrest. Few of them could step back from the appalling reality of the situation: that one female nursery assistant had abused and destroyed the innocence of so many children. It was haunting parents.

In early July a number of the families met with police to be told their children – because of their ages and when they attended the nursery – definitely fitted the profile and were the most likely to have suffered at the hands of George. Parents at that meeting were understandably horrified and some questioned whether it was necessary to inform them in such a vague manner.

One mum at that meeting first noticed something was wrong when her children became withdrawn and began wetting the bed. But she only realized the significance of their behaviour after the arrest of Vanessa George: 'My children meet all those criteria . . . I have to make sure she doesn't affect the rest of my kids' lives. It has been a very emotional ordeal since day one. Every parent's worst nightmare.'

Describing George, the same mother told the BBC: 'If you can think of your average big bubbly woman, that was what she was like. Friendly, lovely, absolutely lovely. The kids love her.' She went on: 'It's the worst feeling you can ever imagine. Feeling sick twenty-four hours a day. Not being able to sleep. Drinking during the day – everyone is the same.'

Even the sight of anyone who looked like George repulsed that mother. She admitted: 'If I see anyone in town who remotely resembles her, I feel sick. And I have to walk in the opposite direction. I just can't cope with the image of her face, because every image is of her smiling.'

Another mother told reporters: 'My daughter asked me why the police had taken Vanessa away. I told her she had been very naughty and tried to explain things to her. She wasn't a direct victim but she has been affected. Her innocence has been taken away overnight. She now thinks it's naughty to be naked. She won't let her father dress her. What happened at Little Ted's will stay with these children for years to come. I don't think that woman will ever realize the effects of what she has done.'

Perhaps embarrassingly, Plymouth police and council officers had still not confirmed whether George had been checked by the Criminal Records Bureau (CRB), although the local authority insisted that anyone working in a 'child-related place' should have been CRB-checked as a mandatory requirement. Meanwhile Plymouth council staff were working with parents who needed to find alternative childcare provision as Little Ted's remained closed for the foreseeable future.

All across Plymouth, there was still a feeling of disbelief about how George could ever have carried out such an appalling catalogue of crimes. Councillor Andy Kerswell, who represented Efford and Lipson, and was also a governor at the neighbouring Laira Green primary school, said: 'I can't believe it. I'm amazed and flabbergasted. Obviously, you can understand every single parent being out of their head with worry at this news. It's easier said than done to ask them to be calm at this time but they need to be calm for the sake of the investigation so they can talk to the relevant agencies to assist police with their inquiries.'

The local minister, the Reverend Martyn Neads, pledged that his Laira United Church would offer support to those who needed it. Part of the church's premises was let to Little Ted's three days a week. The Reverend Neads explained: 'This is a commercial arrangement; the church has no involvement in the running of the nursery and is unable to answer any questions relating to current police inquiries. As a church, we would want to make ourselves available to those who may feel distressed by what is happening, but anyone with particular concerns relating to this case must speak to the police.'

A few brave Plymouth residents continued to try to err on the side of caution, pointing out that George had not yet been tried and convicted. One said: 'Lets just find out if these charges are true before we all jump the gun. Thought in this country we were all innocent until proven guilty? I feel great sympathy with the parents of the children attending this nursery as it may be cause for concern.'

One couple summed up the way the case was affecting Little Ted's families across the city. They had made every effort to ensure their three children were protected from such 'predators' and told newsmen how their teenage daughter, who had also attended Little Ted's when she was young, their eight-year-old son and their toddler had so-called 'stranger danger' rules regularly drummed into them. 'We've always looked at it as trying to protect them,' said their mother. 'My eldest says, "Mum worries too much." She keeps asking me to go to the 11 to 18s disco at Oceana each month. I tell her, "You're having a giggle!"'

The father agreed: 'The other day they all came running into the house saying there was a man sitting in a car down the road. I went to check and said, "Sorry, but my kids spotted you and it's a quiet road and we don't know who you are."' He was really good about it, said he was waiting for a neighbour to come home and well done on my kids for being so cautious.

'We've taught them to be aware, to not go with strangers. They've learned Tae Kwon Do, don't stay out late, they aren't allowed beyond our street. We always keep an eye on them. We did all these things to protect our children, taught them what to look out for. We've been so careful, and still they [a paedophile] got through. That's what makes it so bad, that's what makes it worse. We were giving our children to a paedophile – and then paying them!'

Both parents found the initial news of George's arrest hard to comprehend. 'The first fortnight was hard,' said the mother, whose youngest attended the nursery for two years. 'I did get obsessive. I'd try and take a picture of him, to see how he would cope. I wondered would he be scared, or start posing, or remember something? I started grasping at straws. I'd show him the picture of Vanessa on the front page of the *Herald* and ask him, "Who's that? Is she a nice lady? Was she nice to you?" All he'd say was "That's Vanessa." We sold our family caravan in Looe at once – we couldn't do it any more. We knew Vanessa had a caravan in Cornwall, miles away, but all we thought was "Is there one in this park." That's the time it really hit us. The kids had freedom there. They would go out on their bikes, go to the park area and we wouldn't see them for three or four hours. We could take a break there and not have to worry. Suddenly we thought they were too vulnerable.'

The mother in question said she rarely hung around to talk to other parents or nursery workers, but the father often did: 'I'd always speak to people and so I'd chat to a few staff. The response from everybody was it beggared belief – you just couldn't believe it.' The constant questioning soon became too much for the mum, who also began to recognize how her own obsessive search for the truth was being mirrored by other parents: 'I think that's why I couldn't keep going to the meetings [held regularly at St Paul's church] any more. Otherwise you'd just question and question yourself. Some parents were just talking about it all the time, week after week, going over and over and over it. I couldn't keep going to the meetings week after week. I said to them, "What's the point? You'll just go over and over it and make yourself ill with worry." It can send you mad.'

The father summed up the situation when he added: 'As horrible as it is, you want to know, but at the same time, you don't want to know.'

The mother was particularly concerned about future

problems which could arise from George's abuse, even of the youngest children: 'I've always read a lot about children and abuse cases, and the care system. I've got books about it and I'd read about how people who adopt children are warned that when their adopted kids get older they can sometimes remember things from when they were much younger. The adoptive parents are warned the child could come forward claiming they've been abused.

'What do we do if they come forward saying they remember being abused? What help will there be then? Something could trigger a pocket of memory and how do you deal with it then? What do you do when your child comes to you and suddenly says, "When I was at nursery, I was abused"?'

Two months later, in September 2009, many of the children from Little Ted's would start 'proper' school for the first time since the enforced closure of the nursery. That shutdown was another factor that upset many of the toddlers. One parent explained: 'For the children, they were just yanked away from their nursery and their friends. They didn't understand. Our son keeps talking even now about a little boy who was one of his friends from nursery. He misses him and it's sad he hasn't seen him since.'

At one meeting in Efford, parents' frustrations spilled over into hostility towards some of the Little Ted's staff and they were accused of failing to know what was going on and failing to stop Vanessa George. At one stage during the meeting in a local hall, parents were divided amongst themselves because of deep-set fears about what had happened and why. When one parent suggested letting the children all get together in a local park, and let them all play, groups of parents rejected the idea and began splitting into factions.

One member of staff – popular with many parents – had been to the local unemployment office but was turned away after an official said she wasn't unemployed because she still had the job at Little Ted's but wasn't being paid. As another parent pointed out: 'I feel sorry for the staff. They're all tainted by that place now. Any nursery owner will think, "What are the parents going to think if I employ them." Some parents aren't going to believe anything else, they will think of their own children first and not even discuss it.'

On Tuesday, 7 July, a High Court judge ordered all future court cases involving Vanessa George to take place at Bristol Crown Court. Mr Justice Royce, the presiding judge for the Western circuit, made the decision as he sat at Plymouth Crown Court. In addition, he instructed courts in Manchester and Nottinghamshire that the two other people connected with the investigation centred around Little Ted's nursery – Colin Blanchard and Angela Allen – also have their cases joined with George's and heard at Bristol Crown Court. There was a genuine feeling that Bristol would be a fairer location to try the three because of all the local anger and bitterness in Plymouth.

George had not yet entered any pleas on the seven child abuse and child porn charges laid against her after her arrest the previous month. A statement released by Devon and Cornwall Police confirmed the change of court venue:

'Due to the nature of the investigation, the case concerning Vanessa George will be handled by the CPS South West Complex Casework Unit in Bristol'.

Although the children in George's photographs had still not been identified, by analysing electronic references stored within the images detectives had at least been able to work out roughly when the pictures were taken. With the assistance of a consultant paediatrician, they had also estimated the ages of the children involved.

Detectives then cross-referenced nursery records and narrowed down to thirty the number of families who would have had children of the right age, at the relevant time, in the care of George. But, beyond that, individual identification was proving virtually impossible.

In mid-July police investigators publicly disclosed for the first time that they believed the abuse only took place in the six months prior to George's arrest. They said that contact between George and Colin Blanchard did not start until 29 December 2008. However, despite the police assurances, there were still concerns about George's past and her access to children.

Many parents and staff were aware that George did baby-sitting after school and she attended after-school groups as well as holiday groups. As one parent said: 'It's horrendous. You can imagine the parents who've had her baby-sitting for them at night. Her and their children – just one on one.'

Some parents were starting to genuinely worry that they themselves would go into denial in order not to face up to the consequences of George's actions. One parent said: 'I feel that it didn't happen to our son. What scares me is if the police called and said, "Yes, he was", how would I react?'

The horrors that had unfolded at Little Ted's day nursery increased the anxieties of couples across Britain who, with the aid of the Government, had turned to professional childcare in ever greater numbers over the past decade. According to the National Day Nurseries Association, 15,500 nurseries in Britain cater for 700,000 pupils. Pre-school children spend an average of twenty-one hours a week in nurseries, a study by the Department for Children, Schools and Families found recently.

The chief safeguard was the Office for Standards in Education, Children's Services and Skills (Ofsted). All pre-schools had to register with the inspectorate, which visited nurseries within seven months of their opening and then again every three years. Its most recent assessment of Little Ted's, in February 2008, had found that it provided a 'good quality' of care, with children 'properly safeguarded' from harm or neglect and all staff appropriately vetted by the Criminal Records Bureau (CRB).

It was the responsibility of the nursery owner – be it an individual, a charity or a local authority – to ensure that CRB checks were made. Ofsted carried out further assessments to make sure adequate background and employment histories of staff had been obtained.

Yet George, who had worked for six years as a classroom assistant without raising suspicion, would clearly not have been caught by the CRB net. And the fact that the children abused at Little Ted's were so young meant they could not explain what had happened to them, and made them ideal targets for paedophiles.

While Ofsted insisted that nurseries operated with an adequate child-to-staff ratio and policies to ensure a pupil's dignity, there would always be times when a member of staff might be alone with a child, such as when changing their nappy or giving potty training. Oftsed had the ability to close a nursery that did not meet its criteria, but the watchdog rarely did so.

One Little Ted's parent revealed to reporters how two months before George's arrest, her child came back from the nursery in a distressed state and she had contacted Ofsted – but did not hear back from them. The mother said: 'A couple of times after nursery he was shaking and said he didn't like a particular member of staff. He said, "I don't like her, I don't like her." I tried to get him to explain but he is only two and he can't express himself completely. I didn't know what to do so I contacted Ofsted about the situation but I never heard back.'

A spokesman for Ofsted later admitted: 'We did have one recent complaint relating to Little Ted's nursery. This complaint was not of a level that would require police involvement and did not relate to the content of the allegations made public today. Ofsted is investigating this matter in line with our normal procedures and it would not be appropriate to comment further until the outcomes of that investigation are complete.'

Ofsted was not obliged to investigate such allegations, but officials admitted they would be expected to pass the letter on to detectives or contact the complainant and ask her to contact her local police station. But in this case they appeared not to have done so.

The Vanessa George case had caused a big split in opinions between parents, sometimes within the same house. Many had opposing views on the most distressing, and for many the most vital, question of all: if police were finally able to determine which child appeared in the pictures taken by George, would they really want to know if it was their child?

Many mothers said they would rather not know while the majority of fathers felt that knowing the truth would probably help parents deal with it all better. The future was littered with unanswered questions. As one mother explained: 'We'll have this with us for the rest of our lives. That's why I think life should mean life for her, but she isn't going to get life, is she? Will she have the cheek to come back to Plymouth and carry on her life living here? Will her daughters have any contact with her? Have they visited her? Has her husband?'

There was a mounting feeling of anger and resentment towards what many parents saw as the inevitable 'soft sentencing' of George and her two twisted cyber-friends. Few believed she would really get the heavy sentence she deserved and many wondered if she would ever show any true regret for what she'd done to their innocent children.

Meanwhile a small number of parents remained keen to see the Little Ted's premises reopened in some form as they felt there were many families who needed local nursery education. One mother said: 'A lot of parents still need it

– it's still very much needed by the community. I don't think it could have the same name, perhaps not even the same people, but it's definitely needed. I'm more aware of what to look for now in a nursery. When I put him in at Little Ted's there were times I'd drop him and he'd be screaming and they would tell us, "It's OK, you can go." But looking back you question all the times he was upset. You question if it was normal or something else.'

Nurseries across Plymouth had been inundated with parents anxious about leaving their children in care. Tim Squires, the owner and director of Noah's Ark Childcare Centre, said his staff were absolutely shell-shocked by the arrest of Vanessa George: 'Our thoughts are with the parents, you can't imagine what it is like to go through that type of thing.'

It was, indeed, a horrific nightmare which many of George's victims might never recover from.

17

On Monday, 27 July 2009, George appeared at Bristol Crown Court alongside one of her two co-accused, Angela Allen. It was the first time the two women had ever met in person. The court was told that George and Allen would be asked to offer their pleas on several child abuse and pornography charges at a full court hearing in October. George faced two counts of sexual assault by penetration and two by touching, and one each of making, possessing and distributing indecent images of children.

Allen faced four counts of sexual assault on a girl under the age of thirteen, as well as four counts each of taking, possessing and distributing indecent photographs of children. Both women spoke only to confirm their names before sitting and remaining impassive throughout the short hearing.

George was dressed in a black short-sleeve top and baggy black trousers. She looked down at her hands, occasionally lifting her eyes to watch the court proceedings. Allen, who appeared wearing a dull green zip-up fleece top and blue jeans, spent much of the hearing staring into space.

Their co-defendant, Colin Blanchard, had been scheduled to appear alongside the women but was not produced. Mr Justice John Royce said it was due to 'inexplicable' reasons.

Blanchard, who was charged with distributing, making and possessing indecent images of children, had not been picked up from Strangeways Prison in Manchester, owing to a 'clerical error'. Blanchard also faced one count of possessing extreme pornographic images.

Around twenty people – many of them relatives of the alleged victims in the case – filled the public gallery which looked down on the court. Detective Superintendent Michele Slevin and Detective Inspector Costa Nassaris, from the Plymouth police, sat behind the Crown Prosecutor, Ann Reddrop, throughout the hearing. No officers from Greater Manchester Police or Nottinghamshire Police were present.

Several officers were posted outside the court building as George and Allen were delivered and taken away to their respective prisons. During the hearing – which lasted less than half an hour – the Crown Prosecutor asked the judge for more time for forensic evidence to be collected. She also asked for all three cases to be formally tied together. She said the charges faced by all three defendants were subject to revision and a draft indictment would be served at a later date.

Mr Justice Royce ordered prosecution papers to be served to defence counsel by 25 August. A plea and case management hearing was fixed for 1 October at Bristol Crown Court. All three were ordered to remain in custody.

At Westminster, the Labour Government's Children's Secretary, Ed Balls, reflected the shock of the entire nation when he said it was 'hard to comprehend' how George was

able to 'do such terrible things to innocent children ...
My department is in regular contact with Plymouth [City]
Council, who have been offering ongoing support to the
staff and families. I expect the Serious Case Review by
Plymouth's local Safeguarding Children Board to be com-
pleted as soon as possible.'

George's husband Andrew and teenage daughters Pearl
and Grace announced during the summer that they had
cut all ties with George following her arrest. Andrew
George said he and his family remained shocked and
devastated by the allegations. Initially he had been under
police protection at a safe house after fleeing the family
home with his two daughters but gradually they had moved
back into the family's home in Douglass Road.

'We don't want nothing to do with her,' one close relative
revealed. 'We've cut all ties with her. Andrew and his
daughters don't want anything to do with her, they've cut
her off entirely. We are all totally in shock and devastated.
We never want to see her again. This is a really upsetting
time for us.'

Andrew George had been left shattered and suicidal by
the events of the summer. He later admitted feeling 'stupid
and naïve'. He kept asking himself: 'Why did I never know?'
That same feeling was haunting him over and over again.

He even admitted in one newspaper interview that he
wanted to 'take a s*** load of pills and be done with it, I
feel like that now. But I've got my girls. Painkillers and
anti-depressants, that's how I cope.' In many ways he felt
tarnished and ashamed by what his wife had done even

though it was nothing to do with him: 'People tell me I've done nothing wrong, but that doesn't help.'

Andrew George continued supporting his daughters through their nightmare like any good father. But the fear that fingers might be pointed at his involvement continued. He even made a point of telling one reporter: 'I didn't know anything at all. The police have made it clear that I was never a suspect, but a victim.'

Local friends and neighbours were kind and supportive to his family, though, and he even received a touching card from George's colleagues at Little Ted's nursery, telling him how sorry they were.

Andrew George was also reeling from the few strange conversations he'd had with his wife since her arrest – and her total lack of remorse. She had first called the family house out of the blue about four weeks after her arrest. George announced herself by saying: 'Hi, only me.' Her husband later recalled that she made it sound 'as if she was on holiday somewhere. I was shocked. I didn't expect it.'

After that George called her husband a few times every week but continued to show no remorse. One time she moaned that her daughters had not been in touch: 'I thought the girls would have written to me about how they got on in school etc. I miss them so much.'

But the innocent children she abused were never on her mind – only her selfish demands. She even told her husband in one call: 'Post me a coffee mug I can use. My Starbucks one will do. It would be nice to see my pink flip-flops again.'

Andrew George was astounded by his wife's attitude. Here was the woman he had married and shared a family with and yet she didn't seem to have a shred of conscience about what she had done. He felt as if he had been married to a complete stranger for nearly twenty years.

Six weeks after George's arrest, her husband visited her in prison in Gloucestershire, where she was remanded in custody. He told her he would be attending the sentencing. 'I need closure,' he told her. He later recalled that his wife sounded completely unfazed by her crimes, even commenting to him: 'I'll get four years and be out in two.'

Andrew George never actually discussed his wife's appalling crimes with her: 'It sounds weird but that is how it is. There was never any talk of being sorry for what she had done. For the victims.'

Andrew George knew he had to be careful while visiting his wife in jail not to go into the details of the case as that might prejudice her coming trial. But he couldn't help himself from saying to her she'd done something terrible.

George tilted her head and there was a pause. Then the only thing she said back to her husband was 'Mmmm.' Nothing more.

He told his wife they needed to talk about a divorce but she responded: 'No, not until this is over.'

George was still refusing steadfastly to identify the tots she'd molested – much to her husband's disgust. He wanted her to co-operate with the police and end the torment of the families who still didn't know if their children had been abused.

Andrew George had been completely shattered by many of the revelations about his wife, which were being disclosed to the world through the news media. He'd been stunned by her boasts to friends about meeting up with strangers on the internet. He hated even thinking about her deceptions. He'd heard that she'd taken photos of herself with other men, partly to try to make Blanchard jealous. He'd even received a charge on his credit card for a room George reserved at a Premier Inn in Rochdale, when Blanchard failed to show up.

Mr George allowed the couple's elder daughter, Pearl, to speak in public about her mother. Pearl felt as if she was 'in an invisible steel bubble with my heart as delicate as a marshmallow. When bad news comes my way it penetrates the steel bubble to my heart.' Since the dramatic arrest of her mother, she'd felt more alone than ever but thanks to her family and friends Pearl felt she had support.

Pearl was remarkably calm and mature about what was happening. She knew that none of the rest of her family were involved. She wanted the world to know that and to make sure the people – including her mother – who had been charged were the ones who should be blamed.

Not surprisingly, Pearl was in other ways still struggling to make sense of what happened. George had seemed to be her loving, family-orientated mother but now she was 'somebody else. I think it's pure evil.' Pearl had already decided never to speak to her mother again. She told one newspaper: 'She led a double life right under our noses and kept a dirty secret we knew nothing about. Death would have been easier to deal with because you get over it, but with this it just hangs over you like a dark cloud for the rest of your life.' Pearl then said of her mother: 'Her mind is poison, her smile a plague.'

George's arrest happened when Pearl was in the middle of GCSE exams. The brainy youngster had already sat four key papers at Lipsom Community College in Plymouth when that police raid on Vanessa George's home changed her life for ever.

When police moved the family she was forced to miss other vital exams. But Pearl was determined to sit the exams and go to college to make her family 'feel proud again'.

Meanwhile Andrew George was still hoping to eventually visit his wife once more in prison to persuade her to identify her victims. He knew he couldn't force her to see him but he felt she owed him and their daughters for all the suffering she had caused them. Not to mention George's innocent young victims at Little Ted's.

Gradually, the full chilling implications of the Vanessa George case began to emerge. Many were convinced that George and Blanchard were frighteningly close to abducting a child in real life, which would have put them on a par with the notorious Moors murderers, Myra Hindley and Ian Brady.

The detailed nature of their online discussions implied that George was prepared to do anything to help Blanchard satisfy his craving for sex with children. Privately detectives were expressing relief that they had uncovered the trio's sick and twisted cyber-relationship before a child really was snatched off the streets.

There was even speculation in some quarters that Blanchard might well have attempted such an abduction before he even 'met' George and Allen online. As one psychiatric expert explained: 'These sorts of fantasies can end up turning into reality. Often the instigator tries to get other people to join in so as to "normalize" such acts. In the case of Blanchard, he seems to have spent many years fantasizing about such acts of depravation, which suggests that he may well have tried to commit such heinous crimes in reality, even before he ever encountered these two women.'

In early September 2009 the renowned Scottish scientist Sue Black offered case investigators her pioneering technique to unmask paedophiles who concealed their identity in photographs showing them abusing children. Detectives were still struggling to identify the abusers and their victims from the George case because they were virtually all photographed from the neck down.

Black – professor of forensic anthropology at Dundee University – had developed a technique that could match suspects with the pictures by looking at the unique features of their hands, such as the pattern of veins, wrinkles and blemishes and the shape of fingers and nails. The method had already been used to bring two paedophiles to justice and Black offered to share it with police investigating the abuse at Little Ted's.

The science, developed by Professor Black over the previous five years, had been used recently to identify Neil Strachan, the ringleader of a Scottish paedophile network with links stretching to Australia and America. Strachan – the former secretary of Edinburgh's Celtic East Boys Club – had been arrested after he took his computer to be repaired and a technician found a picture of a child being abused. Police later recovered 7,000 images, including one showing the abuser's hand, which was matched to Strachan's because of a defect on his thumbnail. He was sentenced to life in prison after six of his gang members were sent to prison in September 2009 for a total of more than forty years.

The new science had also been used to identify Dean Hardy, who went to Thailand to abuse children. He confessed when presented with Black's findings and was sentenced to six years in jail. Black believed the method could be used by police investigating the Vanessa George case. 'We're not at all symmetrical,' said Black. 'If you look at the pattern of veins on your right hand and compare it with your left, they are completely different. It's the same for skin blemishes and creases on a knuckle. What we can't tell yet is what the likelihood is of anybody else having the same pattern. This is very much pioneering science.'

September brought its own set of new problems for the Little Ted's parents and many of their children. The case itself had gone relatively quiet during the summer break because the media were restricted from reporting anything until the three defendants appeared for their trial on 1 October at Bristol Crown Court. Thanks to the law of *sub judice*, newspapers and TV could not reveal new developments in case they were deemed prejudicial to the trial.

George's mundane prison existence in Gloucestershire continued without incident, although as she was still kept segregated from other inmates this was hardly surprising. One detective who talked to prison staff during this period later said that 'Vanessa George was by all accounts a model prisoner. She said very little but, bizarrely, always managed a warm smile for the staff.' There were even rumours that George had lost weight inside prison.

George herself stopped sending notes to or trying to phone her husband and seemed to have accepted her fate. She told her lawyers she would be pleading guilty to the charges after being told that she stood to face a shorter sentence than if she dragged out the legal process by refusing to admit her guilt.

As usual, Vanessa George was thinking of no one but herself . . .

18

At 10.45 a.m. on 1 October 2009 Vanessa George, Colin Blanchard and Angela Allen were each escorted by two prison officers into Bristol Crown Court. It was about fifteen minutes before their case was due to begin. Mr Justice John Royce gently warned the parents in the public gallery to contain their 'very strong emotions' prior to the beginning of the 'very sensitive case', saying the proceedings 'must be carried out fully, thoroughly, with proper decorum and without interruption'.

All three defendants sat behind a big glass screen while their respective barristers were at least twenty feet away and none of them would even once confer with them throughout the hearing.

At 11 a.m. all three stood up in the courtroom as the charges began being read out to them. The *Plymouth Herald*'s Carl Eve later recalled: 'As usual, Vanessa George just looked down while Angela Allen looked around, hand to mouth. Colin Blanchard stared forward with a completely blank expression on his face.' The public gallery was packed with more than thirty emotional parents, who wept as the guilty pleas were entered. One man pointed accusingly at Blanchard and was asked to calm himself by the usher.

George, wearing a black T-shirt and black trousers, hung her head as she admitted seven sexual assaults on children and six counts of distributing and making indecent pictures of children. George denied one sexual assault, which was ordered by the judge to lie on file. Blanchard, dressed in a blue sweater and Nike tracksuit trousers, showed no emotion as he pleaded guilty to seventeen child pornography counts and two sexual assaults on children. He also admitted a charge of possessing extreme pornography. Allen, wearing two-tone jeans and a blue jumper, wept as she pleaded guilty to four child sexual assaults and one count of distributing an indecent image.

In the sixteen uncomfortable minutes it took to read out the thirty-eight charges against the trio, and hear their pleas, the parents who had filled the public gallery appeared to run the gamut of emotions. Within seconds of George's crimes being read out, one man ran out of the room choking back the tears, while others sat and wept openly. Women and men clutched each other, some sobbing on the shoulder of their neighbour. Others glared at George, anger and pain etched on their faces, some even standing to get her attention.

However, the mother of two only looked up each time she said the word 'Guilty', not once making eye contact with any of the parents, or her co-defendants, one of whom, Blanchard, she had never met until this hearing.

George appeared unaware of the massive media presence, only offering a fleeting glance at the dozens of national and local reporters sat in one of the public galleries which overlooked the courtroom. Another dozen or so sat on the jury bench while a crowd of photographers and TV cameramen were camped outside the courthouse, many of them having been there hours earlier to snatch a glimpse of the trio's arrival.

Mr Justice John Royce warned the trio they faced substantial prison sentences as he urged George to co-operate with police in identifying all her victims. Mr Justice Royce said many parents still did not know if their child was among the victims. He told her: 'A lot of people are affected by this case and I would like your help.' Speaking to George's lawyer, the judge said: 'Your client must know, it seems to me, who she has abused and who she has not. If I were a parent I would want to know whether my child was abused or not. Would it not be decent for her to indicate who she has abused and who she hasn't? I know from interviews that Vanessa George knows all the parents.'

Parents gave nods of approval as the judge went on to say: 'It's a factor I have to take into account at the end of the day. Has that been considered by you and her?'

Nick Gerasimidis, George's lawyer, responded: 'I am sure Vanessa George has heard your Lordship's remarks.'

The court then heard that Allen – described by police as a 'truly sinister and evil' woman – had minor previous convictions for theft and soliciting, having spent her younger years working as a prostitute.

During the trial, defence lawyers for Allen and George alleged that Blanchard had encouraged the two women to commit abuse. But the judge rejected the suggestions, saying of George: 'She is not a child. This is a married woman who can make up her own mind whether she indulges in this sort of activity or not.'

The judge also pointed out there was an 'enormous'

number of contacts by telephone, email and MSN messaging between Blanchard and George (10,000 from the end of December 2008 to June, when they were caught), which suggested a 'degree of enthusiasm' on George's part.

Detectives insisted the three had egged each other on to share ever more explicit fantasies, abuse very young children and share the images. The court was told how the trio exchanged thousands of texts and dozens of emails, goading each other to commit more depraved acts. They swapped pictures, the court heard, via email using unprotected accounts, including MSN Hotmail, but never met in person. George's job meant she had the easiest access to children. The court then heard that between the end of December last year and June this year she used the camera on her mobile phone to take 124 indecent pictures of children in her care.

All three still maintained they met on Facebook, although detectives privately remained convinced that they contacted each other through a site devoted to paedophilia. The court was told that police and child protection experts had not found images that the three made anywhere else on the internet, suggesting they were not part of a wider ring, although many still believed that the photos must be floating around the internet in some form or other.

Carl Eve noticed that George remained for the most part 'as cold as ice' during the reading out of the charges: 'She was the same as she had been in her previous court appearances. The only time she ever looked up was when she pleaded guilty and her eyes would look up and she would say 'guilty' and then she'd look down again and the rest of the time was spent with her hand either in front of her or at her side fiddling.'

Angela Allen, on the other hand, kept crying as the court hearing progressed. Carl Eve recalled: 'As the charges were being read out, she was biting her finger and then her knuckle.' He noted that when count five of the charges against Angela Allen was read out it made her cry. 'It was strange because after she'd admitted four sexual assaults on a child, one of which was her own child, it was count five when she started crying and that was the charge connected to distributing indecent photographs of children.'

Eve said Blanchard 'just gave off the impression of being a big lump in the corner who didn't seem to care. None of them even looked at each other.'

At one stage, Carl Eve noticed George biting her bottom lip but that was the only emotional response she showed throughout the hearing: 'She seemed absolutely dead emotionally, which was kind of what the police had been telling me all along.'

In court it was revealed for the first time that Blanchard had been on the sex offenders register after receiving that earlier police caution for an offence after the raid on his home by VAT officials.

The court also heard that police believed Blanchard's abuse began in September 2008 and carried on until June 2009. The court was then told how the trio subjected their young victims to humiliating sexual abuse involving plastic golf clubs, sex toys and toothbrushes. But by pleading guilty all three had avoided most of the horrendous details of their assaults being detailed in open court.

The judge then adjourned the case, provisionally scheduling sentencing for 13 November. The entire hearing lasted less than an hour. As George, Blanchard and Allen were led away to the cells, victims' relatives remained calm – except for one man who waved sarcastically and another who ran his thumb along his throat.

Outside the court Detective Inspector Costa Nassaris told reporters police still feared many of the victims – some of whom were between twelve and eighteen months old – would never be identified. But they would continue to try for the sake of the families: 'Work is ongoing, we've not given up on that, but the probability I would have to say is very low that we will identify any of these children.'

Detective Superintendent Adrian Pearson, of Nottinghamshire Police, told reporters that how the trio came to meet on Facebook also remained a mystery: 'How did three people get connected on Facebook and somehow get on to such depraved, awful topics of conversation that led to sex assault of children, betrayal of trust, depravity, awful crimes being commissioned and exchanged between the three of them?'

As to why George abused the trust of others, and the children in her care, one of the investigative team said: 'That's the big question. They'll be lining up outside her cell door for the answer to that one.'

The Crown Prosecution Service's head of complex casework, Ann Reddrop, insisted after the case that identifying the abused children remained a priority for police. 'The CPS South West Complex Casework Unit took on this case at an early stage when it became apparent that any prosecution required all three offenders to be on trial together to allow a jury to understand exactly what they had each done (whether encouraged by one of the others or not) and the judge to sentence at the end of the day also aware of the full picture. Should they have been tried separately around the country, the sheer magnitude of their offending and the amount of contact they had with each other may not fully have been realized.

'Vanessa George's actions left the community of Plymouth shocked. George grossly abused her position of trust. While her victims may be too young to understand her crime, their families do have to deal with those effects.

'It remains a police priority to identify any of George's victims. This has been the hardest element of the police investigation, both for the families and officers involved, and despite the efforts of some of the country's leading specialists in child identification, we may never be able to identify those children.

'The prosecution team will never know what went on in these individuals' minds at the time they committed their crimes but we hope the families involved can take some comfort knowing that all three have been convicted in a court of law today. We must now await the sentences imposed by the court and we anticipate they will reflect the seriousness of the offences and the trauma caused to the victims and their families.'

Ann Reddrop added: 'These three individuals each acted in a way which ordinary people will find hard to understand. They may never have met but between them they committed shocking acts of child abuse. They showed complete disregard for the lives of their victims, their own families and those they worked with, all of whom have been left devastated by these crimes.'

Detective Constable Andy Pilling of Greater Manchester Police's sexual crimes unit said after the case: 'Colin Blanchard's sick fantasies were the catalyst for a chain of events that led to the abuse of innocent children on a truly shocking scale.' He believed that Allen and George had tried to please Blanchard in a 'sick game of one-upmanship'. Pilling added: 'Make no mistake, George and Allen are not victims of Blanchard's grooming. No one forced them to carry out his perverted fantasies.'

Detective Superintendent Michele Slevin, the senior investigating officer from Devon and Cornwall Police, added it was clear George had caused 'massive trauma' to a great number of people. But in a press conference after the courtroom hearing, Detective Superintendent Slevin admitted that despite calling upon experts in identification both in this country and abroad, they had 'drawn a blank at this time', adding that 'we haven't got anybody else to go to.'

Slevin added: 'While her victims are, thankfully, too young to understand her crime, the families of children who were left, in good faith, in George's care have to deal with the effects of her crimes for a lifetime.'

The police believed they could start talking more openly about the case after all three defendants had admitted their guilt at Bristol Crown Court. Slevin told the press outside the court that George had been 'co-operative' – but she was still refusing to name her victims. She said: 'We have interviewed George many times and during these interviews she has been co-operative. Her motivation for not telling us the names of her victims at this time we do not know.

'We have asked her to let on the details which only she knows at this time. Hopefully after the comments of the judge today we will have further opportunity to speak with her and her counsel. Discovering their identities is our top priority. However, despite using a number of specialists and experts from around the country we have drawn a blank. Only she can reveal the names.'

At the end of the court case, Plymouth police insisted once again there was no so-called 'fourth paedophile' linked to the Vanessa George case. There had been fears that another adult might have been involved after an unidentified hand was spotted in one of the images but police said it was unrelated. But officers vowed to interview George one more time in a bid to get some closure for the Little Ted's parents and their children.

On the day of Colin Blanchard's court appearance in Bristol a skip was left outside his house because the new owners were moving in after the property had been repossessed and needed to get rid of any of the Blanchards' belongings still inside the property. Their neighbour Richard Parker takes up the story: 'They had two skips and there were thousands and thousands of pounds' worth of children's toys and they must all have been given to their five-year-old to make her keep quiet.'

In Richard Parker's words, the Blanchard house always

'seemed strange and empty of any personal possessions': 'Since the new people have moved in it now looks like a normal house again with lots of lights on and the sound of life. Before, all you could see was the flickering of the TV screens in every room. It was really eerie.'

Another neighbour said the Blanchard house 'always had the blinds closed. Now perhaps we now why.'

PART FIVE
The Aftermath

'The eyes of others our prisons;
their thoughts our cages.'

Virginia Woolf

19

Andrew George woke up on the day after his wife had pleaded guilty at Bristol Crown Court feeling at the end of his tether. The details that had emerged at the trial had hit the TV news and he dreaded seeing that morning's newspapers because he knew they would be crammed with details of his wife's vile crimes: 'I felt terrible. Worse than usual. I had a lot more on my mind. I knew what I wanted to do. The intention was there. I couldn't take any more.'

Mr George had also just found out that his calculating wife had been siphoning off family cash, leaving him in debt and with mortgage arrears. He couldn't cope. He was signed off work with stress, and for weeks had been descending into despair.

So it was that Andrew George felt compelled to try and take his own life. He knew it would hurt a lot of people, including his beloved daughters. But he felt so desperate that there did not seem to be any light at the end of the tunnel. He took some pills out of the medicine cupboard and started preparing for the last day of his life.

That morning after the trial Andrew George laid out his bank card and Post Office family allowance card in the kitchen, and casually made sure his daughters knew their PINs. He even told them: 'I meant to tell you my PIN codes.' When they asked him why he replied: 'Just in case, you never know.' Then both daughters tapped the codes into their mobile phones.

Andrew then drove his two daughters to school – and on the way back he called at his local Somerfield supermarket, where he bought alcohol and more pills, and a writing pad and envelopes to leave notes. When he got back to the family home in Douglass Road he dressed up to die in a black suit jacket with trousers, a white shirt, and a black tie. He also had a new black overcoat on, to look smart for anyone who would discover his body.

He drew the curtains in his living room, with the small fire switched on, sat on the sofa, his border collie dog Georgie curled up next to him, and put on the DVD of the Hollywood movie *Donnie Darko*. Before taking his overdose, he sent text messages to both his daughters at school. He told them he loved them very much and then said they should go to their grandmother's house straight after school. He didn't want them finding his body. Then he wrote: 'I love you two very much and am proud to be your dad. X X X.'

Then he took the overdose. What saved him was a mobile phone call from a friend as he prepared to write his suicide notes. He answered the phone and heard his friend's voice saying: 'You've got to keep your chin up, mate, you'll get through this.' But then Andrew replied: 'It's too late for that now, I've had enough.' He sounded so drowsy that his worried friend immediately called the police. They arrived at the house within minutes.

Paramedics also dashed to Douglass Road and found Andrew conscious and breathing but in need of 'urgent' medical attention. A spokesman for the South West Ambulance Service later confirmed paramedics had been on the scene within five minutes of the call.

A representative of Devon and Cornwall Police confirmed at the time: 'This looks like an attempted suicide but whether it was a serious attempt we do not know. Alcohol and tablets were involved. Police were called to an address in Efford, Plymouth, around 11 a.m. on Tuesday after concern was raised for the welfare of a man thought to be in the property. Officers arrived and called an ambulance. A man was taken by ambulance to Derriford for treatment. His condition is not thought to be life-threatening and the incident is not being treated as suspicious.'

Andrew George was released from hospital very quickly and the next day emerged from his house none the worse for his ordeal and told reporters: 'I don't really want to talk about what happened yesterday but I feel very good now. This has been the best day in a long time. I have been feeling like I've been carrying the weight of the nation on my shoulders. It has been horrendous, but we're getting through it. People haven't been blaming me for what happened. I just want life to go back to normal now for my girls. The girls are good. I'm not back to work yet but my health is fine and I'm feeling very good.'

He admitted he'd contemplated committing suicide because of the shame he felt over his wife's crimes: 'What I did yesterday wasn't a serious bid to kill myself but I wanted the authorities to realize I need help too and I achieved my aim. I had a long talk with a psychiatrist and afterwards felt like a great weight had been lifted off my shoulders. I'm seeing my GP today and hopefully he will arrange for me to have another urgent hospital appointment.'

Once again Andrew George pleaded with his wife to name her young victims before she was sentenced, to save dozens of parents the torment of not knowing if their youngsters had been abused. He now not only considered his wife to be a 'monster' but he also felt naïve as a result of her crimes. People were wondering how he didn't notice what his wife was doing. He'd also had to face the agony of having to ask Pearl and Grace if they had been abused by their mother. Mercifully, the girls said they had not been.

Andrew George had been clearly struggling to come to terms with what his wife had done. He later said he 'went over the edge' after the police told him that his wife had sent messages to Blanchard which clearly implied they were seriously considering the kidnapping of a child.

Haunted by the image of his wife snatching an innocent youngster, Andrew George was driven to desperate measures. He kept wondering if they would have turned that sick fantasy into a reality. It had seemed so close to actually happening. He later said: 'It was mentioned many, many times, and it was Vanessa who mentioned it the most. They were so close to doing it. That's what knocked me for six. I had no idea she was capable of any of this.'

The emails included that chilling message sent to her fellow paedophile Blanchard from George's laptop as she sat eyeing up children playing at the family's favourite caravan park in Cornwall during a holiday there just a few months earlier.

Andrew George just couldn't get that image out of his

mind. He knew the caravan, the view and even the toilet block well: 'I could picture it as if I was a fly on the wall.'

The messages had been written when George took Pearl and Grace to the caravan park around the early-May and spring bank holidays – leaving him at home. He now realized that his wife simply wanted him out of the way so she could send the girls off playing, and then just sit on her laptop to link up with her sick and twisted Facebook pals Blanchard and Allen. Now Andrew George could imagine his wife sitting there, looking at those children, looking across the park while writing a sexually perverted message to her cyber-lover Blanchard.

The police told Andrew that his wife had even described the caravan site as being 'a goldmine' because there were so many children around unattended. George had also talked about when she was in the loo, in the caravan toilet block, and she came across a little girl who was on her own. He was haunted by the words his wife wrote on her laptop: 'I could have grabbed her. We could have booked a room in a Premier Inn and done what we want. Abuse for our own pleasure.'

On another occasion George had sent Blanchard a similar message after spotting that little boy as he waited for his mum outside a lavatory cubicle at the same Harlyn Sands Holiday Park.

As Andrew George had been recovering in hospital for those few hours following his attempted suicide, he'd also felt deep remorse about what he had tried to do. 'I felt like a p***k to be honest when I looked at all the people around me. There were old people and some poor girl opposite me who had hurt her back or something. I realized how stupid I'd been.'

Another problem for Andrew George was the constant reminders everywhere back at their house in Douglass Road of his previous existence with his wife. He was still sleeping in the same double bed he'd shared with his wife. And in his nightmares he could see her. He'd have visions of her being on the computer, and visions of her turning, and being angry. Then Mr George would often wake up drenched in perspiration with his heart thumping. He was haunted by fears that any kidnapping George and Blanchard carried out could have ended in a killing. 'I think it would have ended up in a death, and maybe not just one either.'

Shortly after this, Andrew George went into therapy and put his suicide bid behind him. He knew he had almost let a lot of people down. His daughter Pearl had been so angry with him, although his younger daughter, Grace, had given her dad a big loving hug.

He admitted feeling 'dirty and ashamed' to have been married to his wife. But he had now promised he would never try and do it again: 'There's light at the end of the tunnel. I know now that I'll come through this OK.'

All Andrew George really wanted to do was ask his wife about what she did. He wanted to know why she'd done it. He felt entitled to know that. His father Bill said his son has been suffering from 'sleep deprivation' since his wife's arrest and had not intended to kill himself: 'He hasn't slept since this started apart from catnaps. He answered the door to the police and they took him to hospital just as a precaution. It had just all built up on him.'

*

New guidelines on using mobile phones in nurseries were finally drawn up by Plymouth City Council in early October, just after that court appearance and those guilty pleas by George, Blanchard and Allen.

The council admitted the council's new guidelines were the result of George's horrifying abuse of babies and toddlers in her care. They were prepared by a range of professionals with 'considerable experience and knowledge' in the field, a spokeswoman said, and both parents and childcare providers would be consulted.

They would go before the Plymouth Safeguarding Children Board at its next meeting and, if approved, be rolled out across the city. The next full meeting was not until the end of 2009, though sub-groups would hold talks before that. However, the list would not include a blanket ban on mobiles in nurseries, and would act as 'best practice' guidelines, rather than strict rules.

Community leaders and senior police officers welcomed the move. Kathy Hancock, chair of the Heart of Efford Community Partnership, called for 'sensible' guidelines, such as depositing phones in a locker or basket before coming into contact with youngsters. 'You can't exactly ban mobile phones but you can learn to manage them,' she said.

Detective Superintendent Michele Slevin, who had led the police operation, added: 'Any measures that are brought in to ensure the safety of children have got to be a good thing.'

A few days after the end of the court case in October 2009 the Bishop of Plymouth, the Right Reverend John Ford, spoke publicly about George and his remarks started much debate because they reflected the opinions of many in Plymouth, although they did also bring the case back into the headlines yet again, which further reminded the parents of the Little Ted's youngsters just how hopeless their situation remained.

Bishop Ford told the BBC news: 'The breach of that trust by this person in such a position of responsibility to me is almost unimaginable.' He spoke as congregations around the city prayed for the families affected by the abuse at Little Ted's. 'Those of us that are privileged by the birth of children know that they are the greatest treasure, almost a gift beyond price. Hard-working parents put great effort into their nurture. Part of that is to entrust them and put this treasure into the hands of others. The breach of that trust by this person in such a position of responsibility to me is almost unimaginable. The parents of those abused must be so fundamentally shaken at this unspeakable wickedness.'

He said that local churches were supporting parents who wanted a quiet place to talk. Parents were 'trying to make some sense of it in an atmosphere of complete dereliction, all caused by this lack of trust. It must be a terrible place to be.'

Life inside prison was proving no bed of roses for George's co-defendant Angela Allen. At HMP Bronzefield in Surrey, she had been so terrified of being attacked that she'd pretended she was on remand for attempted murder before her court appearance on 1 October. One former inmate said that Allen had told prisoners she'd tried to stab a former lover. Sarah Flynn, from Croydon, who served six weeks for perverting the course of justice, said: 'She came up with this story about being a traffic warden and trying to stab her bloke. If anyone had discovered the truth she would have taken a battering.'

Shortly after Allen's false claims were exposed in a national newspaper, and following the publicity from the Bristol Crown Court case, she was attacked in prison by another female inmate. Allen told a visiting relative after the attack: 'I had been taken back to my cell to collect my things. A girl suddenly burst in and jumped me. She called me a bitch and punched me before a guard had to jump in and drag her off.' Allen was left with a black eye and bruising.

Child protection experts across Britain were particularly stunned by the case because it had highlighted that child sex offenders were not only men – and not just people on the fringes of society. It was also a vivid reminder that crimes like this were not just about images, but about real abuse on real children.

By October 2009 Facebook had more than a hundred groups calling for George to be killed while she was behind bars. She had become an international hate figure, with internet sites calling for her to be hanged or 'cut to pieces'. Her name was synonymous across the globe with the lowest form of child abuse and paedophilia.

While there was much wild speculation about the eventual length of George's sentence when she next appeared in court, more details about a possible 'new life' she would be given after serving time began to emerge.

Lawyers predicted that George would probably be given a new home, name and round-the-clock police protection. And many were predicting that as the time for her release approached, her solicitors would apply to the High Court to rule that her new identity and whereabouts could not be revealed in the media.

But they would have to show explicit, realistic death threats for the application to succeed, although she could also use human rights legislation to secure her new identity and twenty-four-hour protection. One of her oldest friends in Plymouth predicted: 'Vanessa will love that. She sees herself as a bit of a celebrity after all the publicity but she knows she's in for a tough time inside prison and an even tougher time when she gets released.'

So authorities were reluctantly admitting that George could well be given a new identity at taxpayers' expense after she was released from jail. George had already received countless threats of revenge if she ever returned to the streets of Plymouth – including a menacing pledge from one angry relative of a child in George's care to strip her skin off and roll her in salt.

The Ministry of Justice would make the final decision closer to the time of her release but it was likely it would conclude there was a serious threat to public order if George were released under her real name. Niri Shan, of the law firm Taylor Wessing, offered the opinion that 'Her lawyers may well try to show her safety is in jeopardy. These orders may be granted in exceptional circumstances, if there is compelling evidence that her safety is at risk.'

So, ironically, it seemed that the threats against her would most likely help George by persuading authorities to give her a new identity once she was released from prison.

George's husband Andrew expressed anger at the news his wife might get a new identity. 'We are also the victims here,' he said. 'She could be found somewhere to live in secret where no one will know of her wicked past and will be able to carry on as if nothing has happened.'

Meanwhile, back in prison in Gloucestershire, George seemed unperturbed by the likelihood she would remain segregated from other inmates – at yet more extra cost to the public purse – for her own protection, and kept under constant supervision. George's lawyer, Nicolas Gerasimidis, said arrangements had been made for her to see a mental health specialist and that psychiatric reports would also be compiled on Blanchard, who spent five years on the sex offenders register because of child porn, and on Allen, who had a series of convictions for prostitution.

Well away from Plymouth and the crimes committed by George, Blanchard and Allen, an almost as shocking case went virtually unnoticed in early October 2009 after a woman teacher was exposed as a 'predatory paedophile' after she sexually abused young children she followed into public toilets.

Carole Clarke, aged forty-six, admitted to police that she systematically attacked boys and girls over a seventeen-year period by following them into public toilets and in total is believed to have sexually assaulted children 100 times.

The offences were primarily committed against young-sters aged between four and seven and she always acted alone, Grimsby Crown Court was told during her hearing. Clarke was a part-time college tutor for adult students at Franklin College in Grimsby between October 2003 and April 2007, and also taught adults from home. She faced a lengthy jail sentence after pleading guilty to six charges. She was remanded in custody and was due to be sentenced in mid-December, the day before George, Blanchard and Allen at Bristol Crown Court.

The court earlier heard that Clarke's assaults dated back to 1992, but she had not been arrested until January 2009, when a health worker raised concerns with police. Besides the 100 offences she confessed to, she also admitted two counts of indecently assaulting a child during or before June 1992 and three charges of sexually assaulting a girl under thirteen during or before August 2008.

One of the sexual assaults occurred in a public toilet in Grimsby's Market Hall, while two others occurred in public toilets in Woodhall Spa. Six other counts of sexual assault, which she denied, would remain on file. Clarke, who was reported after seeking help from mental health professionals, had been on remand since her arrest in January 2009.

Detective Sergeant Stewart Watson, of Humberside Police, said: 'Predatory paedophiles such as Carole Clarke are rare. There are claims that between 5 per cent and 10 per cent of abuse against prepubescent children in the UK is committed by females. However, only about 5 per cent is thought to involve a woman acting alone. There are still those members of the public and even experts who ignore women's capacity for sexual abuse. Thankfully education is challenging these beliefs.'

*

Many people believed that George would continue to refuse to reveal the identity of her victims despite the heartache this was causing so many Little Ted's parents and their children. It was as if she was simply playing for time. But why would she so steadfastly refuse to co-operate?

In tapes of her early interviews with police George had seemed initially willing to talk, even speaking of the motivation for her crimes and the disgust she felt for herself. But as that first crucial interview shortly after her arrest continued, she gradually clammed up when details of her offences were explored, and she eventually became obstinately silent when asked to identify the children she had abused.

But why, if she already knew she was going to prison, did she refuse to give a full account of her crimes? Criminologists believed that a desperate 'power game' lay behind George's behaviour. With every aspect of her existence now at the mercy of the justice system, she came to see the knowledge of her crimes as the only thing over which she had any control.

Apart from thinking about her chances on appeal, she must have felt quite helpless. Undoubtedly she was desperately trying to claw back any kind of power or sense of status for herself. Even minor offenders often become quite uncooperative when they realize they have otherwise lost any influence over what happens to them.

Attention-seeking could also be part of George's motivation. It was as if George realized her period of fame, or infamy, could be extended by withholding such information. That may well have given her a sense of power over the public or the media.

A classic example of such behaviour was the question of whether the 1960s Moors murderer Ian Brady could locate the grave of the missing victim Keith Bennett after more than forty years. When he decided to offer a location to the police it was the only time he'd had some control over the news. Brady's claim that he could still find the grave was highly doubtful. There was also 'nothing in it for him' to assist the authorities, because he had always accepted that he would die behind bars.

In contrast, the co-operation offered by Brady's fellow Moors murderer, Myra Hindley, from the 1980s onwards was motivated by her hope that she would eventually be released. She came clean, made a full confession, and talked about her remorse. She wanted to be seen to be doing everything she could to help the search, in the hope that it might persuade the Parole Board that she was someone who could one day be let out.

Investigators would no doubt hint to George that revealing her victims' names, as a show of remorse, might see her treated more leniently at sentencing or at parole hearings in years to come. Accepting responsibility and understanding her own crimes to ensure the offences would not be repeated would be vital to George's eventual rehabilitation.

The key for the case investigators was to try and find some spark of decency in her personality. They knew only too well that she was trying to keep her true feelings at arm's length, which made things more comfortable for her.

The police detective conducting George's initial, more

open, interview effectively played the classic 'good cop' in order to soften George up and convince her that her crimes, while horrendous, were worth talking about. It was a very successful move until George started to sense that she might be helping sentence herself, so to speak.

That need to maintain an emotional distance from her crimes could explain why George held back from naming her victims. To reveal their identities would involve relating to her victims as individuals. That would personalize the child to an extent and George had done a good job at avoiding that very thing ever since her arrest. As one criminologist, Dr Adrian Needs, explained: 'If you weren't actually thinking about them as individuals in the first place . . . not matching names to particular experiences maybe is a way of preserving some sense of equilibrium and being able to live with yourself.'

Some experts predicted that it might be as long as two or three years before George started fully recalling the details of her horrendous crimes. 'With some individuals you can almost get this kind of paralysis – it's almost as if it's too much to take in,' added the criminologist.

Others still hoped she might 'see sense' and begin to help the Little Ted's parents, children and staff begin to achieve some level of closure. George needed to accept that what she had done was appalling. She had to come to terms with being exposed and that her life would never be the same. For the moment she was being labelled a monster and that was probably forcing her to remain in a state of denial.

So, following that Bristol Crown Court appearance in

October 2009, George continued to close her ears to the outcry from parents of boys and girls who attended Little Ted's nursery, despite their anguish and the fear that they would never know if their children were among those abused. Even George's husband and his parents had echoed the trial judge's call for her to do the 'decent thing' by identifying her victims.

It was impossible to know whether George would ever name her victims.

The police in Plymouth, meanwhile, had become well aware that by being more open about their efforts to get George to tell them the names they had effectively made things harder for the Little Ted's families, because every time the police spoke to the press, it resulted in more headlines which caused pain and anguish to the victims' families.

So the police went back to being much more tight-lipped about their efforts to get George to reveal her victims' names. They had also become perfectly aware of a real danger that they could end up being used as a pawn between the media and George, who in many ways seemed to be enjoying all the publicity surrounding the case.

Detective Inspector Costa Nassaris, head of Plymouth's public protection team, warned: 'We haven't ruled out everything as far as our investigations are concerned, but she could end it now, by telling us the names of her victims. However, we would still try to corroborate it, because there is always the concern, can you ever trust what she says?'

The police in Plymouth decided to go ahead and push for another interview with George, in which they would try to prise the truth out of her once and for all. DI Nassaris confirmed that talks with George's lawyers to set up the next interview were imminent. George's legal team, headed by her defence counsel, Nicolas Gerasimidis, were more than happy to co-operate.

Days later came a surprising breakthrough. Or so it seemed.

The *Plymouth Herald* crime reporter Carl Eve was told by a contact that George had finally started disclosing the names of some of her victims. The source close to George's defence team claimed that the names of at least ten abused children had been passed to Devon and Cornwall Police via her lawyer, although George was still refusing to speak to officers directly. Detectives were trying to check the information using George's photographs before even considering whether to confirm identities to the anxious parents.

The police insisted that none of the identities had been verified, although a senior officer did admit that some names had been passed on to them. A police spokesman said at the time: 'As part of ongoing inquiries, detectives are involved in a dialogue with George's defence counsel, and the question of victim identification is part of that. It would be inappropriate to go into this further until sentencing is complete. We continue to update parents regularly. Currently, no individual children have been identified and this information confirmed, but we continue to investigate this.'

Naturally many Little Ted's parents immediately demanded to be told whether their children had been abused, although others had already decided they would rather not know. Some parents remained convinced the children were too young to say what had happened to them and were unlikely to remember in the future so they weren't even sure if there was a real point behind this line of inquiry.

George was no doubt hoping that if she did co-operate properly it would be reflected when she was sentenced. George claimed she'd told her defence team everything she knew, but some people were far more cynical about her motives in 'coming clean'. One parent said: 'She's despicable. She's only doing this to save her own skin.'

Some parents accused the police around this time of failing to keep them informed of developments. Before the disclosure of George's alleged 'confession', the only recent communication from police had been a letter apologizing to families for failing to notify the parents of a BBC documentary on the case. One mother who suspected her son had been abused said: 'I am disgusted because we have found out everything through the media. The police have been no help whatsoever. These are our children at the end of the day. The group meetings when this first happened were useful but you can't talk about the possible abuse of your child in front of a hundred people.'

Like so many parents at Little Ted's, this mother was blaming herself for failing to spot the warning signs of abuse in the first place: 'Your child is screaming and kicking at nursery and you don't know why. My son came from that nursery staring into space. He has now started school and is developing and thriving well but something happened to him. A mother knows. I just hope she has been honest and is finally telling the truth.'

Other sources tried to insist that George really had genuinely 'confessed' and had told her defence team everything she knew. One source was reported in the *Plymouth Herald* as saying: 'We are looking at double figures in terms of the number of victims she has identified. She obviously wanted to wipe the slate clean so she can get a lighter sentence.'

But detectives remained sceptical about George's so-called 'co-operation' and one police source in Plymouth said: 'Now she has named names and is no doubt hoping that will be reflected when she is sentenced. She told a family member from jail that she may get four years – and serve only half that in jail. But she may be in for a big shock – we think the judge will add another ten.'

Certainly, her 'ploy' in beginning to reveal names initially had the desired effect when her trial judge, Mr Justice John Royce, agreed to put back her sentencing hearing by a month – until Tuesday, 15 December – after the judge conceded that George's 'co-operation' meant that officials needed to allow more time for material to be gathered. The same old dilemma existed for all the Little Ted's families. As Mr Justice Royce commented: 'If they don't want to know, and I fully understand why some parents should not want to know, then the information should not be thrust upon them.'

20

By the end of October 2009 the news that George had finally given lawyers the names of some of the children she abused had appeared in virtually every media outlet. But still the police remained sceptical about her co-operation, pointing out that she definitely hoped it would guarantee her a shorter custodial sentence.

In her prison cell, was George gradually and finally starting to 'crack'? Maybe she had at last begun to face up to the enormity of her crimes? Or was she just cynically trying to manipulate the system for her own benefit?

Police and lawyers who met her at this time believed she had lost her hard edge. They said she looked more broken, as if the reality of facing a much heavier sentence than the four years she expected had finally dawned on her: perhaps the ten years some were predicting for her and Allen, while their male 'ringmaster', Blanchard, could end up with an even longer term in prison.

Back in the George family home in Douglass Road, Andrew George seemed to be well on the road to recovery after the shock of his wife's arrest and conviction and his subsequent suicide attempt. At the end of October 2009 he began a romance with a pretty blonde neighbour called Sharon Blackmore. Within two weeks she'd moved into the family home he'd shared with his wife until just a few months earlier.

Sharon had actually held a torch for Andrew for many years but a chance encounter just sixteen days earlier had changed everything. While walking to the local fish and chip shop, Andrew George had spotted her getting off the bus and decided to talk to her.

Sharon knew all about the arrest of Vanessa George and asked how things were for Andrew and his daughters. He said they were getting better, and that he and his children were doing OK. The pair swapped mobile numbers and began texting each other as soon as they got home.

Two days later, after a night out with friends, Sharon visited the family house. Andrew later recalled: 'I didn't want to sound forward but I told Sharon I don't sleep that much any more, I'm up late all the time, so she can feel free to come over. She did, and we talked, and had the most wonderful time. We ended up talking all night, and cuddling. It was really special.'

A week later Sharon, who had been engaged three times before, moved into the house in Douglass Road and joined the family. The couple then began apparently working through Andrew's troubles. Racked by memories of his wicked wife, he found his sleep was often disturbed by nightmares.

Sharon was equally open about her feelings for Andrew, admitting she had always 'fancied him'. But she'd never told him before because he was married. Now she wanted to be there for him and she even told one newspaper: 'But life goes on, and I couldn't be happier.'

A few weeks earlier – when he had tried to commit suicide – Andrew George had been on the verge of giving up on life but now Sharon was helping him and his daughters find a way through the wreckage of their lives. He genuinely believed that his new lover was making his family feel 'complete for the first time in many years'.

Sharon even explained: 'I don't care what Vanessa thinks, it doesn't bother me at all. Andy doesn't feel he owes her any respect at all, after what she's done. I agree.'

Now Andrew George and his new love found themselves clasping hands at every opportunity., He went on: 'This has been incredible – I'm in love and I've never been happier.' He told friends he was just waiting for his wife to be sentenced, so that he could get divorced and marry again. He added: 'After what Vanessa's done she can rot in her prison cell.'

He continued to denounce his wife's belated move to co-operate with the police as a self-serving bid for leniency. Pouring scorn on reports that George had finally, after weeks of defiant silence, identified ten of her young victims, he insisted: 'I've been told by the police that it's NOT 10 names, it's six. And then it's only first names, not full names. It's an empty, token gesture. It's nothing really. The police have still got to find out who's who, and what was done to who. Vanessa's just playing around. She's getting off on this, and she holds the power card.'

All of the headlines proclaiming George's so-called 'confession' now looked a bit thin.

Andrew George was particularly angry because he believed his wife knew the name of every single child she'd abused. And she was well aware that she was putting all those parents through hell: 'Yet she's giving just first names of six. Why doesn't she just hand over the full names, so the parents that want to know, can know?

He believed his wife was revelling in the attention and wasn't in any way interested in the feelings of the Little Ted's families: 'She's a bitch, and she's callous. Perhaps this is a last ditch attempt to try to get a lesser sentence. She's convicted now and she realizes that she's going to be put away for a long time. But this is too little too late, and I hope the judge sees right through it. I hope she goes down for as long as possible.'

He planned to be in the courtroom to watch his wife being sentenced in the hope it would bring some closure for him and their two daughters. His 'new love', Sharon, even pledged to stand alongside her lover in court in December, when George was expected to be sentenced.

For the first time since his wife's arrest, Andrew George was trying to move on. He'd cleared out boxes of his wife's belongings, and planned to redecorate the entire house to erase the memory of their sham marriage. And Sharon had also quickly formed a close bond with his daughters as a substitute mum: 'The girls give her a kiss every morning and before they go to bed. She sometimes has tears in her eyes, and tells me how great they are. They all go shopping together. They get on so well.'

Andrew's elder daughter, Pearl, who'd earlier announced that she could no longer bring herself to call George 'Mum', genuinely believed that Sharon had filled the gap left behind. She loved having her around. 'I thought we'd lost Dad when he tried to kill himself, but Sharon's helped him to pull himself together.'

Andrew George was still receiving counselling sessions to help put the trauma behind him and believed that his new life with Sharon was the key to his happiness. Meanwhile he was still waiting for his wife to sign a visiting order to enable him to go and visit her after her conviction: he'd given her times when she could phone the house, but she had not been in touch. He wasn't even sure whether to expect to speak to her ever again.

While many were highly sympathetic to Andrew George's plight, there was a feeling of surprise that he had decided to move another woman into the George house so quickly, although it's virtually impossible to equate that to the shock he must have suffered after finding out about his own wife's sordid secret life.

Whatever Andrew George's motivations it's impossible to fully appreciate the pressure and strain he was under from the moment his wife was arrested. Everyone reacts in different ways to a crisis and, all in all, Andrew George seemed to be handling his family's problems in the best way for himself and his children.

Devon and Cornwall Police eventually conceded that the list of names George had finally given to them was being 'painstakingly investigated'. Officers intended to compare the names with previous statements and interviews, as well as photographs that were seized from George's computer, before even considering informing any parents.

A police source close to the investigation said: 'No one

in the team is going to take anything she says at face value. This woman is a criminal who has lied before and will no doubt lie again.' He warned it could be days, if not weeks, before any parents were told their children were on the list. On hearing the latest development, one parent commented: 'Everyone feels like they were completely duped into trusting her every day with their kids, so why should we trust her now? We've all seen the interviews with police, when she refused to comment. We've seen her in court when she refuses to look anyone in the eye. Why should we believe a single word she says now?'

At the beginning of November, George wrote a letter from prison to her husband in which she apologized to her two daughters, saying: 'I know I have let them down.'

George said she realized Pearl and Grace hated her but she pledged to 'explain things to them when they are older'. In the letter, George conceded that she knew her daughters did not want to communicate with her but she pleaded with her husband to tell them that she loved them and missed them. George admitted she knew she had let them down and even asked her husband to 'be strong Drew and be there for them, you know what I'm talking about.'

But, typically of George, she also asked her husband to make sure some of her clothes were sent to her in prison and expressed no concern for her victims or their families. She even whined in one section of the letter: 'I am not very well.'

George's letter asked for her favourite black hoodie top, 'the one with the stars on', a selection of V-neck T-shirts, and a pair of flip-flops. The obese fiend even demanded some black knickers, 'size 18–20'.

Then, incredibly, ignoring the breakdown of her relationship with daughter Pearl, George asked: 'If she has an old pair of black trainers kicking about, can I have them please?'

Andrew George told the newspaper after handing over the letter: 'She should be wearing sackcloth and ashes after what she's done, not dolling herself up.' Andrew said he had no intention of running round his wife 'like a housemaid, gathering up underwear and clothes. She won't need to look fashionable where she's going for the next few years.'

On 29 November 2009 Andrew George disclosed publicly that both he and the police believed his wife was such a dangerous paedophile that police were planning to ask the court to issue a life ban on her contacting children . . . including her two daughters. Plymouth police intended to ask the trial judge at her fast approaching sentencing hearing on 15 December to impose a far-reaching Sex Offences Prevention Order (SOPO).

Her own family had backed the police application for the order blocking her access to kids, including vulnerable adolescents like her daughters Pearl, fifteen, and Grace, thirteen – even while she was behind bars. The order would have immediate effect if granted. Whether it was a life ban would be up to the judge but the police fully intended to press for it to be so.

SOPOs – first issued in a paedophile case in 2004 – usually came into force when a sex offender was released and banned contact with children for a maximum of five years. The offender could also be banned from using computers and mobile phones with internet access. Breaches of the order carried prison terms of up to five years.

This one against George – if granted – would be the toughest yet handed down and would mean Pearl and Grace could have no contact with her at all until they were eighteen – even if they wanted to see her.

Andrew George had urged police to push for the ban after receiving the letter from George begging for her daughters' forgiveness. He considered his wife to be a highly manipulative, scheming woman and he was genuinely worried about the mind games she would try to play with their daughters over the following years.

The George case's senior investigating officer, Detective Superintendent Michele Slevin, had even written to parents of George's victims at Little Ted's revealing the Devon and Cornwall force's intention to apply for the ban. 'I hope that by the time Vanessa comes out of jail, the order will have teeth and that she is properly shackled,' wrote Slevin.

Slevin also confirmed that George's much publicized 'confession' about the names of her victims was not as significant as had at first been believed. She added in her letter to the parents: 'Not all are full names, some are just first names. We will need to interview Vanessa George again.'

So, for the moment, George was behaving in exactly the way those who knew her best had feared. One relative explained: 'Vanessa is incapable of putting herself in the place of those poor parents and their children. She's been stringing everyone along and now the police are going to have to start all over again if they want to try and establish who she really did abuse. It must be so dreadful for those families although I am sure Vanessa doesn't give a damn.'

In prison still awaiting sentencing, George was finding that her so-called 'celebrity status' meant being surrounded by guards for virtually every waking moment. One inmate who came out of the same prison in Gloucestershire at the end of November 2009 said that George was 'banned from even speaking to other inmates'. According to the ex-inmate: 'It's weird, really, because she is treated like royalty in a sense but then there are so many inmates who'd like to take a pop at her just to improve their own reputation inside.'

And both inside and outside, it was being predicted that the authorities would 'make an example' of George and give her a very heavy jail term at the sentencing on 15 December.

The day before George faced her sentencing on Tuesday, 15 December, her husband Andrew told one newspaper: 'I want her to look at me from the dock – if she's got the guts – fix me firmly in the eye and see for herself her family's hurt etched on my face. She has cruelly betrayed, humiliated and shamed me and our daughters. Some people pointed an accusing finger at us, suggesting we must have known what she was doing, but we never had an inkling and were shocked as anyone else when the scandal broke. Vanessa has torn so many of our lives apart, but so far she is oblivious and indifferent to our pain, or the seriousness of her crimes.

'Now I want her to make a last gesture, one I think me and the girls deserve. That is for her to look me full in the face, to see for herself the distress she has caused us through her black heart, poisoned mind and wicked ways.'

Then it was revealed by her husband once more in the *News of the World* that George had taken a naked photo of her *own* daughter Pearl getting out of the shower a month before her arrest. She had waited on the landing with her cameraphone and even mocked: 'Tee hee, got yer!' as she scurried away.

Then following her appalling 'ambush' George even wrote a sickening caption about fifteen-year-old Pearl for other child sex predators to read. In it she fantasized about the teenager – making what one policeman called 'disgusting comments of a sexual nature'. Then, unbeknown to Pearl, the photo was circulated to fellow fiends Colin Blanchard and Angela Allen by George.

Pearl bravely spoke out about her mother's ultimate betrayal, just forty-eight hours before George was due to be sentenced for her crimes: 'I want people to know why I really hate and despise her so much. A mother is supposed to be there for her daughter, isn't she? Not betray her. What she inflicted on those unfortunate babies and toddlers at the nursery was wicked, but to then discover she had no conscience about exploiting me, her own flesh and blood, was awful.'

Pearl added: 'Some people, including my friends, couldn't fully understand my hatred and loathing for her, and thought I was being too harsh by disowning her. Now I hope by talking of the lengths she went to to use and embarrass me after I took a shower, people will accept why I'm so bitter. At the time I didn't tell anyone about it. I was too shocked and embarrassed. But she could see how upset I was. I dismissed it as a one-off incident, which she'd never try again. She said it was only a joke. In the context of what she was later accused of, I realized I'd never be able to trust her again.'

At Little Ted's nursery, workers were upfront and honest about their attitude towards George now the full extent of her evil deeds had been revealed to the world. Her co-worker Isaura Coburn said: 'Words can't describe how much I hate her. Everyone who worked with her is haunted by the way she wormed her way into our lives. She was always obsessed with sex. She even publicly fantasized about having sex with the dads who dropped off their children at the nursery and flirted with them on Facebook. But using the children in our nursery as sexual objects? How could any woman be so depraved? I feel sick every time I think about it.'

Since George's arrest, her twelve co-workers – who'd lost their jobs when Little Ted's was shut down – had desperately tried to work out when the abuse could have taken place. But the awful truth was that George was alone with children on thousands of occasions. During nappy changes or toilet visits, she had ample time to fulfil her depraved fantasies.

Isaura described how 'Some of the younger girls saw her as an authority figure and tended to let her take the lead even though she wasn't supposed to supervise. But generally, there was nothing unusual about her behaviour with the children . . . it wasn't as if she was touching them inappropriately or taking every chance to be alone with the kids. We were always very careful about looking for bruises or changes of behaviour, thinking – ironically – it might be a sign of problems at home. But there was nothing untoward.'

It was also disclosed on the eve of George's sentencing that many of the names in her so-called 'confession' to the police did not correspond with those of the children on the nursery's attendance register on the relevant dates.

*

On Tuesday, 15 December 2009, George finally appeared in court to be sentenced. In an emotional five hours at Bristol Crown Court, she sat just yards from the parents, who were joined in the public gallery by her husband.

Throughout the hearing, three of the Plymouth mothers subjected George to an unflinching glare, never once averting their gaze. George, flanked in the dock by Allen and Blanchard and three guards, shielded her eyes from them by holding her hand to her face or hiding beneath her long, lank hair as she stared at the floor.

Some of the mothers and fathers wept as the prosecutor, Simon Morgan, told the judge, Mr Justice Royce, that George had admitted feeding the lust of her Facebook accomplice with sick pictures of children in her care. The court was told how George was obsessed with IT salesman Blanchard, telling him she was his 'paedo whore mumma'.

The judge described the evidence as 'chilling' as he heard how George and Blanchard discussed raping, abusing and photographing children in the 'grotesque' text messages they sent each other.

Police admitted that the scant detail she gave to them might never enable them to identify which children she assaulted at Little Ted's. The judge revealed that child protection officers had visited 180 children thought to have had contact with George.

Mr Justice Royce told the court: 'A small number of children were displaying worrying signs which may be symptomatic of sexual abuse but it was not possible to know.' He said that, for the parents, not knowing whether their child had been violated was 'the hardest aspect to deal with'.

He said to George: 'Parents have to live with the memory of you coming out with a smile on your face to hand back their child, when you may well have been doing unspeakable things to that child.'

Staff at Little Ted's, which has now closed, said they felt 'betrayed' by George's actions and one said that 'a lifetime of childcare had been ruined by Vanessa's actions.'

The defence barrister, Nicolas Gerasimidis, said George was 'caught up in a double life' where she both cared for children and was abusing them. Counsel for George and Allen claimed both were vulnerable and eager to please. They claimed the majority of the pictures showing objects penetrating their victims were staged. Blanchard had promised both women love and attention and a future together, and manipulated them to serve his sexual needs.

But Mr Justice Royce said George's barrister had made her abuse sound as forgettable as 'a cup of coffee'.

Simon Morgan, prosecuting, confirmed that George had declined further police interviews to reveal the identities of her victims. Mr Justice Royce said there were so many doubts about what George had told police it was not possible to identify the children accurately: 'It would be quite wrong for the Crown to tell parents that their child had been abused if in fact that was not the case. I find it difficult to accept that she is genuinely not in a position to provide more information than she has.'

George had earlier admitted seven sexual assaults on children and six counts of distributing and making indecent pictures of children. Allen had pleaded guilty to four child sex assaults and one count of distributing an indecent image.

Blanchard pleaded guilty to seventeen child pornography counts and two sexual assaults on children. He also admitted possessing extreme pornography but the court was told that he might face further charges so his sentencing was adjourned.

The prosecutor, Morgan, described how George became obsessed with sex and even commented to a child's father that his boy was 'well-endowed': 'Witnesses believed her sexual boundaries had blurred. It was as if she wanted to do anything to please Blanchard.'

In the judge's words: 'This was wicked, cold, calculated, repeated offending which for any decent person defies belief.'

The judge eventually gave George an indeterminate sentence for 'plumbing new depths of depravity' by abusing those innocent children in her care. Her co-defendant Allen was also given an indeterminate sentence, but would be allowed to seek parole after five years.

Mr Justice Royce stressed that he was passing 'in effect a life sentence' and explained to the court that George could end up staying much longer in jail than she would under a life sentence, but he admitted that she could go before the parole board after serving just seven years.

The judge explained that he was bound by sentencing guidelines and that imposing an indeterminate sentence was not a 'judicial whim': 'I cannot emphasize too strongly that this is not a seven-year sentence. It is emphatically not. It is, in effect, a life sentence.'

George seemed to nod as the judge said: 'If the parole board is not satisfied it is safe for you to be released then you will spend the rest of your days in prison. Some may say that would be too harsh. Many, and I suspect everyone so deeply affected by your dreadful deeds, will say that would not be a day too long and is no more than you deserve.'

Death threats were shouted from the public gallery as George was led away from the courtroom after she was sentenced. Inside the court, mothers screamed abuse at George. One called the punishment 'a joke' and stormed out of the court in disgust. Another lunged towards the dock and threatened to kill her.

Angry parents of her victims stormed from the building, with one shouting about the sentence: 'You get more than that for robbing someone's house.' Another mum said: 'There should be hanging for this.'

Parents said they were 'disgusted' by the ruling and were considering whether they could appeal against it. Many of them pointed out that they also face a lifetime of torment as George took the secrets of her 'wicked, despicable crimes' with her to jail.

In a joint statement the families of George's victims said after the sentencing: 'Since that day the police first came to us we have gone through every emotion from anger and hatred, to the guilt as parents we now all feel. We are no longer able to trust people whom we once relied on to care for our children and this feeling could last a lifetime.'

In a statement released after the hearing, George's husband said her arrest six months earlier had plunged his family and the parents of babies and toddlers at Little Ted's into 'a nightmare that continues to haunt all of us'. And he said he 'bitterly regretted' her refusal to reveal the full names of her victims – despite pleas from parents and her own two children: 'Such callousness illustrates the contempt and complete indifference in which she holds all of us.

'I hope the doctors and psychiatrists who will be treating her in prison will be able to unlock her twisted mind in the hope of curbing or curing her addictions in preparation for her release. In the meantime, I hope the woman who has betrayed so many lives for her own gratification will find a shred of decency and ease the ongoing heartbreak of so many of us.

'I now plan to divorce her and begin a new life with my new partner, who has become a real mother for the girls. I sincerely hope that all the others affected will in time also be able to move forward with their lives.'

Afterwards media commentators tried to make sense of what appeared to be a relatively short minimum sentence of seven years. The outrage and bewilderment at the sentencing was understandable

But the answer seemed to lie in the Government's controversial sentence of Indeterminate Public Protection, and the arcane rules which accompanied it. Effectively, it was at least as harsh as a life sentence, as it carried the possibility the offender would never be released.

Indeed, lawyers for both George and Allen begged for their clients to avoid the punishment. But, in the way it has to be delivered by a judge, it could not have been more confusing to the families of victims. Initially, the judge had to state in court the maximum sentence he would have passed had he not been considering the indeterminate sentence he ultimately gave to George and Allen.

When all George's offences were tallied up, this gave a total of twenty-one years – including fifteen years for her crimes of penetration of numerous children with an object, and six years for the making and sending of indecent images to her paedophile accomplice. For Allen, who abused one child, the total sentence was calculated at fifteen years.

By law, because the pair had pleaded guilty at the earliest opportunity, Mr Justice Royce then had to apply a hugely controversial edict from the Sentencing Guidelines Council that their sentences must both be slashed by a third, leaving George with fourteen years and Allen with ten.

Next, he was then compelled by law to treat the pair as if they were receiving a fixed-term sentence, and halve their punishment. That is because all prisoners are entitled to be at least considered for release once they reach the halfway point.

The judge – acutely aware of how this would sound to the families of the victims – remarked: 'Members of the public will ask why do you have to do that? Again, it is not judicial whim. It is because in effect Parliament says I must.'

But this does not mean that either George or Allen will be released when their minimum term is up. Instead this would merely be the first point at which they could even be considered for release. And for as long as they pose a danger to the public, they will remain behind bars. That would not be the case had they been given a fixed term of fifteen, twenty or even thirty years.

But none of this appeased the families of George's

many, innocent young victims. She had effectively handed out her own twisted life sentence on them and so many people when she broke those parents' trust and decided to abuse their children.

Just a week before Christmas Day, 2009, George sent greetings cards to her two daughters – who immediately threw them away in disgust. The identical cards showed a jolly cartoon snowman and were marked: 'To a special daughter'. George addressed older daughter Pearl as 'my darling Pearl' and then wrote: 'My pink pearly princess with your eyes so blue. Please remember I will always love you.'

She described her youngest daughter as 'my gorgeous Grace' before writing another excruciating verse: 'With your jelly baby ears and cute button nose, I love you from your head to your toes.'

The two teenagers branded the cards as a 'sick joke' and George's husband Andrew said: 'This highlights the delusional world she inhabits. The girls see her as the Devil.'

Epilogue

The *Plymouth Herald*'s reporter Carl Eve witnessed the Vanessa George story unfold at first hand and his unique insight into the case provides another angle on the entire story. Eve – a one-time crime reporter on the mean streets of East London – had moved with his family to Devon in the belief it would be a safer environment for his young children. He was the first reporter to be told of George's impending arrest and earned a well-deserved reputation for being one step ahead of most other journalists on the fast-moving story. He commented: 'This case has rocked Plymouth to the core. I myself have two young children and it makes you question so many aspects of life.'

Eve said he doubts if Plymouth will ever fully recover from the shock waves caused by George's monstrous behaviour inside a children's nursery: 'The then Chief Superintendent described the Vanessa George case as a "critical incident" not just because of the crime itself. That was quite straightforward but it was the impact on the community and what would follow on from it that was their main concern. And don't forget that at the beginning nobody knew how far back they were going to have to track. They knew she had been doing childcare for ten years so she could have been doing it that long, and remember, this is a city that went through William Goad (see page

302), the multi-millionaire who abused hundreds of children. Goad created a generation of problem criminals in the city by abusing them. He created this mini-underclass and effectively destroyed their lives. He shared some of these children with other paedophiles. Then along comes another one [George] who is in childcare and she's been in the "business" for at least ten years. This sparked more panic in Plymouth. They had no idea. I have kids of that age and we were worried there are women in those nurseries and any of them could be a paedophile and panic set in over that.'

Carl Eve then provided a unique 'take' on how the case itself unravelled. The day before George's arrest, Eve had been informed by one of his police contacts that an arrest in connection to the Little Ted's nursery was impending. 'Then the morning of her arrest I was told by my police contacts to make sure I was in. Vanessa George's name had been bandied around from that night of the raid and closure of nursery.'

Within hours, Eve had got confirmation of George's name from three separate sources and his picture desk at the *Herald* had even managed to dig out some photos of her which had been taken at a local event ten years earlier. 'Finding that photo was an amazing piece of luck. It was in our own archive from 1998 and she was surrounded by children at another nursery. She had darker hair and a chubby face.' That photo was quickly picked up by the national newspapers and TV news programmes around the world.

Carl Eve summed up the perversity of what George had

done perfectly: 'Here is a woman who works in a nursery and has even taken a course on child abuse and how to spot it. I believe she even used what she learned on that course to try and "play" the police after they arrested her. The tragedy of all this is that I still believe that George actually fell in love with Colin Blanchard and was prepared to do anything for him and that's how she got pulled into his evil web.

'Yet I have also seen some of the police photos of what she did to those babies and it seems incredible that anyone could do that in the name of love but somehow I really do believe that is the case although it in no way excuses what she has done.'

Eve also witnessed the reaction of George's husband Andrew to the unfolding story of his wife's appalling crimes: 'I feel for the poor guy in many ways but he's a bit out of his depth. Now he looks like he is in some ways cashing in, but I suppose no one can blame him since he clearly had no idea what she was doing until the police turned up at his front door.'

Just after his wife's Bristol Crown Court appearance on 1 October, one of Carl Eve's colleagues at the *Herald* went round to talk to Andrew George at the family home and was greeted with a sign on his front door saying that any media inquiries should be directed to his 'media agent', the veteran tabloid journalist Tom Hendry of the INS News Agency.

When this author visited the George family house in Douglass Road, Efford, on Tuesday, 27 October 2009, Andrew George answered the door but immediately handed out Hendry's phone number and described him as 'my agent' and said that all inquiries should be made to him.

Ironically, Carl Eve and his fellow reporters at the *Plymouth Herald* had initially decided not to try and interview Andrew George immediately after his wife's arrest. 'We felt we should be sensitive and back off. My approach was let him get through all the chaos first and then we will speak. Then the next thing we know he's signed up with the *News of the World*.'

Carl Eve added: 'He's been feeding the *NoW* line after line since her arrest. He's been well briefed to keep things going through his agent.' Within weeks of George's conviction, Andrew George's agent had sold half a dozen big stories to the *News of the World*, earning in the region of £10,000 in the process.

Eve believes that George must have 'airbrushed her previous life' before she met Andrew: 'It's almost as if she had no life before she met him and he has made few references to her family before she met him.'

The *Herald*'s Eve was also the first journalist to locate and interview Colin Blanchard's work colleague who first spotted the child sex images on Blanchard's work computer and then alerted the police: 'He told me Blanchard was the kind of guy who would do anything to show he could do something. He would brag about it all. At one stage Blanchard had even claimed he was downloading child sex images just to prove he could but of course he had been nicked in the past for the same sort of offence so he obviously was into it.'

The tenacious Eve only managed to track down Blanchard's Manchester work colleague after stumbling on a blog site where people were commenting on the Little Ted's case. 'There was this one blogger who called himself "The General" and who seemed to know quite a bit about the case so I contacted him on the blog site and asked him to pass on my details and eventually both Blanchard's work colleague and one of the Little Ted's parents came back to me.'

Eve continued: 'It took a few months of sending messages back and forth but I eventually got him to talk to me after convincing him I wouldn't shaft him. His own work colleagues had sold their stories to the press. He lost a fortune over this case because anything connected to Colin Blanchard businesswise he had to drop completely. He had to dump loads of contracts and stuff that had been instigated by Blanchard.'

Certain aspects of the Vanessa George case still irk Carl Eve to this day. 'Blanchard was cautioned and only got put on the sex offenders register for five years after that original incident when police raided his house. I have seen so many paedophiles being given the same sort of deal and then they walk out of the door and survive and go back to doing it all over again.'

Eve has his own theories as to why George was 'tempted' by Blanchard. 'I guess it's something to do with women of a certain age and a certain look. She was about to turn forty. She was horrifically overweight. It's almost as if she decided she was on a knobbing frenzy trying to pull other men. She even showed pictures of them off at the nursery on her "fun" phone which she'd snatch back to make sure no one saw the "other" photos of those poor children being abused. She no longer romanced her husband like she used to. It really was a classic. Her daughters had turned into teenagers and they'd found their own feet. She was sitting there in a duff job in a duff home thinking that this is all shit and then along comes Facebook and she can connect up with people. In Facebook she found a group she wanted to be a part of and then along came Blanchard taking the same route he took with all the other women. He made them give him their MSN address or home email address and off they went. It was as easy as that.'

Eve added: 'George clearly got into a rut in her marriage. As the police say, "She got bored of her husband and went off hunting." The internet is perfect because you don't have to show what you look like. Even her husband admitted life had got a bit dull.'

The reporter was stunned by the few friends she seemed to have in Plymouth. 'They just never came out of the woodwork. I think people were ashamed of knowing her or they simply didn't know her. She seems to have gone through life with very few friends. She drifted around from relative to relative after her mother died and even when she was alive, her mum was out a lot and she must have had an exceptionally lonely childhood.'

But Carl Eve predicts that the aftermath of the Vanessa George story will linger for many years in Plymouth. 'She's damaged the very core of the city. It's taken many batterings in its history, including a lot of Hitler's bombs, but the pride has been knocked out of this place by what she's done. It's quite simple really. She was in charge of looking after people's children. She was entrusted with that responsibility and she not only failed but tried to turn some of those children into her sexual playthings just so she could impress a man whose sexual habits were beyond redemption. No one held a gun to her head and made her abuse children and then send the images to Blanchard.'

Because of the position of trust held by women like Vanessa George, it is thought that many similar cases may well have gone unreported in the past. The Child Exploitation and Online Protection centre (CEOP) – which helped police investigating the abuse by George, Allen and Blanchard – has commissioned studies into the behaviour of female sex predators.

The centre concedes that obviously female sex offending is perceived as rarer and more shocking than the male equivalent. A spokeswoman explained: 'It's difficult as a society to accept that women can be capable of those crimes and be sexually motivated to commit them. The way we think of women as carers of children, it's hard to conceive they could be capable of treating children that way.'

The number of female offenders is hard to quantify but 'more and more' are being identified as a result of raised awareness and some experts believe it could be 20 per cent of the total. And it is believed that the number of female offenders will increase.

There are marked differences between male and female offenders. Women, for example, will use the internet to talk in forums but don't tend to collect pornographic images. That said, female offenders can have a worse effect on a child because of the destructive impact which abuse can have on the way children form attachments to others. It has a particularly severe impact when that perpetrator is a woman.

Tragically the children that women most often abuse are the ones closest to them. Women are less likely to be predatory in their criminal behaviour, according to Detective Superintendent Graham Hill, who works at CEOP. He heads the Behavioural Therapy Unit and specializes in interviewing female sex offenders: 'Predominantly the female sex offenders we know about offend against children they know,' said Hill. 'They offend in a controlled environment. They tend to stay close to home.'

And they often also tend to stay close to the internet. It appears that, while sexual offending most certainly predates the development of the internet and digital photography, the emergence of both have made offending easier. 'These people have always had a sexual interest in children,' said Hill. 'But the internet validates and fuels those existing beliefs. And it puts them in touch with like-minded people.'

So the internet is undoubtedly affecting the pattern of offending in this area of criminal behaviour. Sherry Ashfield, from the child protection charity the Lucy Faithfull Foundation, is one of the few people in this country who has spent time talking to convicted female offenders. She has seen an increase in the number of women who use chatrooms to meet like-minded adults and then go on to use the web to share obscene and illegal material.

Ashfield has been able to build up a profile through her research. Although she stressed that these women do come from a wide range of backgrounds, and vary in age and personal histories, 'they all have very complex personal histories, often with complex issues and experience of abuse,' she said. 'They tend to be women with low self-esteem, women who are socially isolated, and who find dealing with emotion extremely difficult. They tend to have a history of depression.'

Their motivation varies too. Ashfield's research suggests that while some women will abuse to please or keep a partner, others will abuse to meet their own sexual needs. Some may also abuse for money: 'We have had women who have had debts who have met someone on the internet who has suggested that if they would take part in making abusive films or pictures of children they would pay them significant sums,' she said.

There is no simple answer as to why women do it. No clear trigger either. While I was writing this book one of my relatives asked me why, when there is so much beauty in the world, must I explore such an ugly case? And here is my answer: everyone I interviewed while researching this book told me how important it was that we examine George's crimes and force the truth about her out into the open.

So the Vanessa George case is far from exceptional. The number of children reporting sexual abuse by women to the UK charity ChildLine has more than doubled over the past five years. Latest figures show a 132 per cent rise in complaints of female sexual assaults to the helpline service, compared with a 27 per cent increase in reports of abuse by men.

Historically, of course, it has been hard for society to accept that women abuse children at all. This is something which makes it even harder for boys to come forward and speak about what happened to them. As one male victim said: 'What chap, regardless of age, wants to admit his abuser is a woman? It's not something that men will readily admit to. It implies you are a wimp.'

Following the case of Vanessa George, the traditionally held image of women as carers and nurturers, incapable of behaving in such a despicable fashion with a child, has been challenged as never before.

'Years ago, people were very shocked to hear that children were abused at all,' said Diana Cant, a child psychotherapist who works with the victims of female sexual abuse. 'The same is now true about female sex abuse. People can hardly bear to think about it or get their minds around it. We want to push it away. It flies in the face of the image of mothers as carers.

'It's important for people to realize that it does happen and, as we do that, it becomes easier for survivors to talk about it. Many children go through life believing they are the only people to whom this has happened. There's an enormous therapeutic benefit in realizing that they are not alone. For it to be more publicly recognized is enormously important in helping people get help.'

The true scale of the problem is as yet unclear. It is

thought that high-profile media cases – such as that of Vanessa George – will encourage victims to speak out. There is an over-riding feeling that when the public hear a story being told they feel they're not alone, and they then feel less isolated and more able to talk about something which is a hugely taboo topic.

Cases such as Vanessa George's seem to highlight a deepening moral crisis that hangs over modern Britain. The bonds of ethical responsibility that once held our society together appear to be dissolving, or so many believe.

Physical aggression is endemic in our society while restraint has been replaced by a brutish eagerness for immediate gratification or money. Most disturbing is the growing incidence of violence within relationships, a worrying proportion of it perpetrated by women.

The traditional feeling that marriage is a place of safety and mutual support seems to have evaporated. Instead, in too many partnerships, marriage has become an engine of competition and loathing, with the most lethal consequences. Many believed that the George case was a sign of a worrying trend in which women were becoming as dangerous as their criminalized male counterparts.

Yet it is vital to maintain a sense of perspective. There have always been evil, vicious women in our society. Violent female offenders are nothing new. The late-Victorian age, for instance, was horrified at the revelations of the crimes perpetrated by Mary Cotton, who murdered four successive husbands, partly for money and partly because she wanted to start a new sexual relationship each time. She was also believed to have murdered several children. When she finally went to the gallows in 1873, she was suspected of having killed at least twenty people.

And one should never forget that one of the worst serial killers in British history was the nurse Beverley Allitt, who murdered four children, attempted to kill another three and caused grievous bodily harm to a further six while working at a Lincolnshire hospital.

Then there were notorious offenders like Rose West and Myra Hindley. So, from a historical perspective, there is nothing actually unique about the offences to which George has confessed.

It should also be noted that in the recent glut of so-called 'misery memoirs' – where adult writers recall the horrors of their childhoods filled with physical and sexual abuse – the worst offenders in these books often turn out to be women.

Again, in contrast to the traditional gentle female image, the figures who lurk on these pages are savage matriarchs or brutal mothers, their menace all the more terrifying because of their gender.

But today in films, television and a lot of literature, there also seems to be a worrying emphasis on gratuitous violence, such as that in the notorious *Saw* movies in which a sadist plots how much torture to inflict on his victims.

The internet – which featured so prominently in the George case through the use of social networking sites – has played its malign part, tearing apart the social and geographical boundaries that once held immoral behaviour in check.

Online, everyone is the centre of their own imaginary universe. But, sadly, imagination sometimes spills into reality, as grotesque fantasies are enacted.

The Facebook Connection

Facebook is just five years old, and over 300 million fans worldwide claim it has enhanced their lives immeasurably. But Vanessa George, Colin Blanchard and Angela Allen have reinforced fears that there is a darker side to social networking.

Facebook allows you to create your own profile – a way of feeling important and individual, when your life could be very different. In fact, many users create a tissue of lies, which new cyber-friends will never know to be untrue. It's about whatever 'face' you decide to adopt online.

George had created a completely different character for herself, as had the two other convicted paedophiles in the case.

Facebook has 'clubs' that anyone can join – most of them are pretty harmless. But other Facebook groups are more sinister. Cyber-bullying is on the increase, with tragic consequences – only recently Holly Grogan, a fifteen-year-old schoolgirl from Cheltenham, committed suicide by jumping off a road bridge because of the horrible messages she had received on her Facebook page.

The 'Facebook Connection' is the one aspect of the investigation that detectives have continued to fail to resolve to their satisfaction. Colin Blanchard, Vanessa George and Angela Allen claimed they met on the social networking site some time between September and December 2008. But the police don't know how they managed to discover, on an open social networking site, the sick and perverted desires they had in common. Unlike on other similar sites, most users' Facebook pages are by invitation only and advertising an unhealthy interest in young children is likely to attract unwanted attention.

Police have warned that this is the style of modern paedophilia today – abuse kept at a distance by people whose desires are fomented on the web using false or hidden identities. It also highlights the 'other' side of social networking: bringing together like-minded people who, rather than old school friends, are paedophiles.

Detective Superintendent Adrian Pearson, of Nottinghamshire Police, said: 'The thing that puzzles all the professionals in the hi-tech crime world is how on earth did three people meet on Facebook? It is accessed by millions of people, yet they somehow got on to such depraved awful topics of conversation that led to sexual abuse of children, betrayal of trust and deprivation. The sheer unlikeliness of these three people being connected in that way will be a puzzle that will go on. In any event those three have willingly shared images, texts and fantasies of the most serious level imaginable.'

Today Facebook is discussed in every playground, workplace and pub in the land and lets friends stay in touch across the globe at the touch of a mouse. But detectives are mystified as to how the worlds of these three strangers could collide on the website. Investigators have trawled the trio's internet traffic but are still none the wiser.

Angela Allen posed on Facebook in a see-through top and boasted she thought of sex '95 per cent of the time!' She listed her political views as 'shoot 'em all!' At the time of her arrest her 'profile' picture was of a hand pushed down into a pair of scarlet knickers.

A psychologist, Graham Jones, said: 'The attraction of Facebook stems from us being social animals – it allows birds of a feather to flock together. We all love being in groups and Facebook lets us do that.'

Jones said the arrival of the internet has made it easier for people to commit child sex offences. He added: 'The internet provides much easier access to other people with similar feelings.' But at least technology has also made it easier for police to trace offenders.

When carefully questioned by police, all three independently insisted they had met on Facebook. But surely they would have been noticed had they tried to use Facebook to find like-minded people? It may be, some police investigators believe, that they met in a chat room and used Facebook after that. They did not use Facebook to move images around: that would have been too risky.

Whatever the truth, police are sure that George, Blanchard and Allen's 'operation' was not particularly sophisticated. The trio made little attempt to hide their tracks and the texts and emails they sent left a trail for police to follow.

One of George's few tricks was to have two phones – her 'fun phone' that she used to take the images of abuse, a second for her 'normal' life. The faces of the children she abused were not shown in the pictures – the main reason they cannot be identified, a common tactic for abusers.

Huge puzzles remain. Where did they meet if it was not on Facebook? Could there be other victims? Were they part of a wider network? Police have found no evidence that the images were spread further than this bizarre, closed gang of three. Software that allows them to search for the images across the internet has not thrown up matches to suggest they were sent to a wider audience.

So, for the moment, many questions remain unanswered and it should never be overlooked that if Colin Blanchard's work colleague had not stumbled upon all those depraved images then all three would still be abusing children and swapping images to this day.

William Goad

The Plymouth sex beast William Goad was the city's most notorious paedophile until George's crimes hit the headlines in June 2009. Goad was jailed in 2004 for a series of heinous sex crimes which shocked the nation. The total number of crimes he committed is as unknowable as the damage he did to two, perhaps even three, generations of Plymouth residents. Goad raped children in his home, his warehouse and his van, on camping trips and in a cottage on Dartmoor, buying their silence with drugs, money, sweets and toys, and threatening violence if they told anyone.

He admitted fourteen specimen counts of buggery, the first of which dated back to 1965, and two of indecent assault. He also pleaded guilty to obtaining a false passport in 1998, when police launched their investigation. Goad had already been taken to court three times for indecent assault, but was put on probation and sent on a sex offenders course in 1972, while in 1980 and 1987 he received suspended sentences.

Goad was sentenced to life on 4 October 2004. He was described in court as a 'voracious, calculating, predatory and violent homosexual paedophile' who boasted of beating his own 'record' of abusing 142 boys in a year.

A great many of Goad's victims found solace in the bottle or the needle, or in extremes of violence to others and to themselves. Some took their own lives, no longer capable of living in emotional and psychological agony. Their parents, brothers, sisters, partners and children have suffered with them.

A special support group had to be set up to deal with Goad's victims and it has received around one Goad-related referral a week since he was jailed. Goad tore his way through vulnerable, emotionally starved young boys. One, who lived in abject poverty, later admitted to police he cried the first time Goad hugged him as he had never been shown such kindness before.

Others marvelled at the open house policy which saw teams of youths hang out, drinking pop, eating snacks, and playing table football or pool at Roville, one of Goad's homes. A self-made millionaire, Goad created an empire which was an alluring trap for his victims. Selling items at knockdown prices, he would happily help out struggling single mums, even offering jobs to their young sons. He created the Mount Gould Camping Club, which he ran himself, encouraging young boys to join.

Staff noted how Goad, as a former director of Cornish Market World, which still houses Ben's Playworld, one of the largest indoor children's play parks in the South-West, would happily sit and watch the children play for hours at a time. He owned two houses in Plymouth – in Tavistock Road and Ford Park Road – both overlooking school playing fields.

Another predatory Plymouth paedophile who was part of Goad's group that attacked teenage boys was jailed for fifteen years in 2006. Peter Norsworthy, aged sixty, of

Taunton Avenue, Plymouth, Devon, was found guilty on all thirteen counts: nine of rape, three of indecent assault and one of intimidation, all on males under the age of sixteen between 1992 and 2001.

He was sentenced to fourteen years for eight specimen counts of rape, four years for one count of rape and one year for each of the three indecent assaults, with all the sentences to run concurrently. He was also convicted of intimidating one of his victims and sentenced to twelve months, to run consecutively. His time spent on remand of a year and 109 days will count towards the sentence.

Timeline of Evil

2002 Colin Blanchard given a police caution by Greater Manchester Police for possession of indecent images of children. He'd downloaded images from the internet – not generated by him. He was then placed on the Sex Offenders Register between 2002 and 2007.

December 2008 Blanchard 'meets' Vanessa George via Facebook and they begin an online relationship.

Early 2009 George 'meets' Angela Allen and together with Blanchard they form a three-way cyber-sex relationship.

1 June 2009 Blanchard visits Unit 10, Wheel Forge Way, on the Trafford Park business centre, in Manchester, and uses one of the company computers to access his Google mail account. He forgets to log out.

5 June 2009 The businessman owner of the unit finds the Google mail account still open and stumbles upon numerous sexually explicit images of children. He calls Greater Manchester Police.

Rochdale CID, on behalf of Greater Manchester Police, executes a warrant to search his home.

6 June 2009 Blanchard is arrested at Manchester Airport as he gets off a flight from Dubai, where he was on a business trip. An Apple iPhone and laptop are taken off him by police and sent to the force's hi-tech crime unit. They reveal numerous indecent images of children aged around twelve to eighteen months. Many of them are said to be 'new' and 'in the public protection arena'.

Blanchard is interviewed by child protection officers at Rochdale Police Station. He admits the images came from a Plymouth woman called 'Vee George'.

8 June 2009 Blanchard is charged with various child sex offences.

'Vee George' is identified as Vanessa George. One of the photos in Blanchard's computer shows her wearing a top with the Little Ted's emblem, although it is partially obscured because the picture shows George lifting it up to expose herself. But by checking pictures of other people on her Facebook page, police are able to clearly identify the nursery.

8 June 2009, 6.40 p.m. Devon and Cornwall Police informed by Greater Manchester Police of their find. Plymouth officers work through the evening, gathering information and preparing warrants.

8 June 2009, 11.55 p.m. Officers from Plymouth police knock on George's door in Douglass Road, Efford.

9 June 2009, 12.05 a.m. George is formally arrested at her home.

9 June 2009, 12.30 a.m. Police interview George at Charles

Cross Police Station, in Plymouth. It is the first of four interviews to be held with her during that day.

9 June 2009 The investigation is labelled a 'critical incident' and named Operation Morley by Devon and Cornwall Police (it is later changed to Operation Hopton after another nursery with the name 'Morley' complains).

A specialist police team is brought in for searches of the nursery and George's home. Computer experts begin a careful examination of George's equipment because 'flash drives which contain information can be disguised to look like anything these days – like a Lego brick or a lighter.'

George's holiday caravan in Harlyn Bay, near Padstow in Cornwall, is also searched.

Police seize mobile phones – a Samsung mobile phone and a Sony Ericsson mobile phone – and computers from George, all of which contained images of child abuse at the Little Ted's nursery and text chat and other 'sex-chat' of a disturbing nature which have been forwarded to Blanchard. Police eventually conclude there is 'no evidence' that the images have gone outside the three.

Blanchard appears at court in Manchester and is remanded in custody.

10 June 2009, 12.43 p.m. George is formally charged with a number of offences involving sexual abuse of children and indecent images and makes her first court appearance in Plymouth.

16 June 2009 Greater Manchester Police identify another woman – using the name 'Ang Bank' – from Blanchard's computer. They discover extreme images of her abusing a young girl and she is identified as Angela Allen.

17 June 2009 Angela Allen is arrested at her home by Nottingham Police along with two men. Investigators find emails from her to Blanchard fantasizing about the rape of a child, and of getting other men involved to carry out multiple rapes of the child.

Allen is charged with sexual abuse of a young girl, as well as making and distributing indecent images of a child. The arrested men are released and cleared of any involvement.

20 June 2009 Allen makes her first court appearance in Nottingham.

30 June 2009 Blanchard is produced from prison, re-arrested and interviewed. He admits offences, including taking photographs of himself abusing a young girl and then forwarding them to George.

27 July 2009 George and Allen appear at Bristol Crown Court, but no pleas are entered.

1 October 2009 All three appear at Bristol Crown Court and plead guilty to the charges.

15 December 2009 At Bristol Crown Court, George is sentenced to a minimum of seven years and Allen five years.

Acknowledgements

I cannot begin to express the depth of my feelings for the many individuals who've made this book possible. I owe them my deepest and most heartfelt gratitude.

To my editor Dan Bunyard and his associate at Penguin, Paulette Hearn, I say many, many thanks. Without them this book would never have been possible. Their support and guidance have been very much appreciated. A special word of thanks to Tammy Cohen, my esteemed and highly talented research executive, who helped 'knit together' a lot of the background on George's catalogue of awful crimes. Then there are Bob Duffield, Barry Medway, Carl Eve, John McShane, Roger Marks, Richard Parker, Frank Highland, Dave James, Jordan Reynolds, Jason Gould and William Annersley, plus many other friends and associates of Vanessa George, Colin Blanchard and Angela Allen who would rather their names did not appear here in print.